BICYCLE

BICYCLE

ROBERTO HARRISON

NOEMI PRESS
LAS CRUCES, NEW MEXICO

Library of Congress Cataloging-in-Publication Data
Harrison, Roberto, 1962-
  [Poems. Selections]
  Bicycle : poems / Roberto Harrison.
     pages ; cm
  ISBN 978-1-934819-40-1
  I. Title.
  PS3608.A78375A6 2015
  811'.6--dc23

                          2015003999

Book Design: Steve Halle
Cover drawing by the author from the series *Red and Black Cluster of Beings*

Published by Noemi Press, Inc. a nonprofit literary organization.
www.noemipress.org

for Brenda

beyond this book
more light
because of you

Resistance assures that all the wheels are turning, that the eye sees us, that potency is a delegated power dropped upon us, that it is the nonself, things, coinciding with the darkest self, with the stones left in our waters.

—José Lezama Lima

TABLE OF CONTENTS

REFLECTOR

los ojos de nieve

an endless line
of arrival,
crosses again
the shores of a lake—

a moon
that's hard
and shiny
with stretched skin.

a death revolves
as breathing gives
its round, and Ready
lit OFF, beside
a bloom

of blackened feet
and wings.

the casket
full of faces
and hands
that leak,
an oiled bird

saddled
with dominion,
sits
& serves a beam
that shatters,

flattened
and divided

along each
parched and brittle
Step

a sun for the saddle

the stitch
along a rounded
home, is curved.

the wind reels in,
magnetic fields
are rising

through the summer
filled with fur.

its evening swells
and softly turns
each loop
above the mouth
and memory
of wood,

in alleys
leading to the light
that others read—

a wooden door
makes calls
that oxen

and an elephant
outside the water
in each eye
Return

a land of coconuts
and tapirs
inches
through the hatred
that a promise
in the giant fence
of letters...

a knowledge
in a target
filled with ruins
and a swamp
in handshakes

alibis—
its privileges
like eggs,

a cell
with inclines
of a city
in its calibrated
season, like the friendly
face of daylight
in a burnt down city
under deserts

filled
with clowns.

this is a twilight
for a shoulder
that is gone

in storms
of owls returning
to the continent
from snow, the size
of other countries
being measured
like a dress
for walking
through the peace
that marks the sun
with circles,

with a radio
that fear reduces
to a pack of city
lives, with cuts
inside the woven hand
that children save
by oceans
full of incubated
selves, and cold,
they wave,

a test
that bodies bleed
to shiver
in the rice
that feeds its highway
to the other side
unknown to some
revolting mouth

it's one that comments
for the ice
and one that serves
to filter all the holes
in caves
that icons
fold, outside of spines
and bloated stores
of weapons

surfacing
its face
to undermine
a home
for ants that others
build, instead of air
outside the night
of dim replies

there is a skeleton
that knots each song
inside the word

that settles
fast devices,
in the shower
ridding
all the brothers
of the kite
that kills the sky,
without a string
to pull
lagoons
inside a gathering
of younger piers,

it's separate—

a will, a knife, a door,
and covered glass
as clear
as rain

with links
between the things
and selves
together
with a seeing
that dissolves

song for Saraha

a midnight
shower
of the roundness
of the sea, a drum
that pulls
the starfish

to an entry
filled with foam
replies, like slices
making fire
of crowded space,
like phases
of a memory
that holds
a bridge—a rock

for towns of empty
stalls, the horse
that carries princes
to the arrow
moved around
inside a wall.
days will empty
each relation

for the salt
of sea–like
wavering

its face
like burning mountains
in the price
that moves outside
an icy sound
in rivers
full of color
for the spine
and ashen tent
of seeing

it removes
the arm
when keys
that do not turn
rewrite
the music
of a deer
inside

it resolves
the visit
to the executions
at the fair,
and other
doors
that magnify

the sold
undone
as one

a linear
encircled
trounce
can weave the shores
into the fountain
that a butterfly
will wave
with crowds
and stealing
in the dragnet
of a pool
of doubt

its secret folds
intend another
rest
to make the tip
return
the air, the aim
puts down a mote
to welcome
Mexico
and forest flowers
that entrust
the eye
with blackened stars

a radio
without a space
reports
the widened
force of daylight
to the pocket
of a window
in the flesh
of walking
through the word
as made
with an encampment
that the porch
sits on

a ride
that twists an oven
in each palm

a reddened husk
that follows all
the microscopic
lines of straw
makes circles
move

to fit remainders
like the hummingbird
that peels its face
outside the two
inside a point

returning
for the corner
that is never there

a light in sounds
that curve
along the canyon walls
and make the calling
ancient spider leave
for onions that are small
and ripples
that increase
the floors of dirt
for things.

it spirals
all the salt
to cheer
the serpents
that a shirt returns

to weave the rings
pronounced
outside the beeping
dust
that letters
might embrace
and willows
wave into the lines
of automatic
errors

in the face
of screens
outside the air
that elevates
the clouds

space for another

the pulse
of flecks of skin,
like shards
that ravel
all the groups
of tables left to lift
into a fly
filled mouth,

says to gifts as one
with wheels
of nighttime exhalations,
a hill
in each that sees
a hill

to wear a skeleton
with silent exits
in a coupling
and string
of moves in longer
visits, to the motor
and the wick
that does what dolls
can see

in every door
a hand intends
to open
in the segment
that a coat
and winter know

sure as others
in the vein
of valid paints
and steeping
in the heat that poisons
each reply, the data
swollen
with surveillance,

like the largeness
of a server
and the empty ride
of never going
for the valley
in the sun

with an alternate
that comes
with salivating
dogs, with tin
that builds a road
remembering
a number

for the plans
that level
each remainder
like the dolphin
that a swimmer loves

a face of greenish
trees and stashing
pictures
that magnetic veils
reveal in flecks
of light that angles each
reply

with granite, steel,
and fleshy bulbs,

the spring
that does not know
percentages, the aching
solvent that the mouth
makes more of, like apologies
and moving
for a bridge

is making tunnels

is what others

is the weave

is shuttling and sparked

•

is a beckoning

the peel

when sleeping
like a twin reflected
for a siren, and the whole
that makes a writing hand
a palm, with whittling
and willows
breaking
through the soil
that levels
each
that levels
out
the city

on the time that fills
the back with mornings
in a rain
that breathes an isthmus
under specks
of circling
like horses, like a letter
that the daylight counts
outside the coin

WHEN a practice

WHEN a listen

WHEN a clouded lung is emptied

WHEN assemblies are light

an ocean charges
through the door
and many roads
remake the beaches
of arrival
of a split
and pier that reaches
fish, outside
the sand and snow
that parking lots
make tolls together,

breaks in services
like slaughter
that the head
and background
sing along

as plastic holes
can see

eleven

"the equality
of all
that lives"

no?

a trembling fixedness—

the earth
unwinds a sentence
in a field
of wooden spheres,

a shower
from the rainbow
plows the heat

an open door
lets air
pass through
another
without windows

a park that moves
Escapes

remains outside
the life
of bodies,

another place
in weather
that a shore
might draw

a person full
of toggled
chalk lines,
carves
from what will live,
those that were
to follow
by the planet
of a fire
resemblances, wheels
that are too thin
to turn, a tunnel
through the calcified
derision
of a see-saw
visitation—hear

because the moment
of a 3 pronged
loss can be
a start, the stung
will never side

with carnivals
that mask the canopy
of repetition, full
to wear a vent, a face
together
with a button
and a husk
belongs to wind
tonight

metal disk,
a heart to heavy
tin,

canyon sides,
a double
on the Western most
connection
to the snake
that pulls its own
from oceans,
from the few,
a hammock
in the sky
for some

a plate
before the phase
to follow traffic
on the rise,
is underneath

the door
and sounds
to stay the still,
to center

on a street

rain cannot
track others
to the hook,
a pole of better waves
with hands, it falls
like shirts, remote
to slide
in alleys
on the sun filled corn
of sitting, rows

belong to lots

Atlantis

feeds the color
in a show
of stools,

a grave
for finishing
the most
that memorizes
swelling ice
alone

a music
for the still
revolving face,

American,
i bleed

the claps
and tunnels
in a velveteen
projection, a bomb
to face again
with onions
in the gasoline
that sits
like pools
to shrink

a lung

mary of oceans

tree lined
target
left

in a flattened field
of wrecks.

cutting through
a waterfront

to give,
the ice
passes

clicks—

a cell
pleads

for soil
of florid
coffins

open out
the trapped

lip lined
trellises,

a monster
that a lie
moves through,

in social
crevices

quiet
in the rain,

a place
to grieve
for palms,

a burst
of salt

a self
of negative
intent

ways
to find
a song

an i—
duration

the others
fall, like
days
in parts
of noon
eclipses

toward
a blank.

surrender
to the home
that moons
resemble

in a faded
view
that peels
the lack
of skin

an eye
that starts

a mouth
that heals

a body
tent
that rivers
send

a marker
that is true
like softened
pores
of traveling

the sun beside
another shore

its lineage
a double
seed

a circle
more
than things

it's not the bullet
that a float
will find alone

it's the hole,
the possible

anyone
that sees

in false
revolving faces

that a promise
calls another,

a prop
that reads its
suicide
with countless drops

a planet
that the sold
will give

to see the shapes
that make a toy
out of the tears
that wet
an end, that i
cut over
to receive, in this

that places all
the planets
on the phone,
that makes the tunnel
like incisions,

in the surfaces
that place
a mind without
a road to give

the pleasing
dust
that makes
a road
remember

what horizons
are what others
place, in terminals
a solid
wall
of death, in

the place that makes
another way
connect outside
a cycle
full of muses

i am proof
that America
will die

ritual number

the 3 of rooms
for a space
in the caravan
that a thinning
horse
sleeps through

the 3 of faces
that a river bleeds
for fish, alone

the 3 for 4
in words
that stretch
a gown
equating, it's a motor
from the smiling
vision
that extends
the firing squad
for seeing

the 3 for 4
in one
without a semblance

that a rowing makes,
a 2
under the wave

a 4 for seven
that beside yourself
makes many
for the hearse
to come
for children, flat
on locked down plains
they fire out
feet
of repetition

a seven for an empty
view, or the sea
that never reels
the beds, on the clotted
pulse
that a mother
bombs

an eight that every
eye
interrogates,
the continent
for countless clouds
in the aftermath
of earthquakes

the one unknown
for 9, the hands
for planting each
in ruins
that a flower
spreads
to see
the night

the 10 because
a 7 knows, in
each removal
that a winter
solves to wear,
under a tree
that many sell
for younger suns

eleven on
a click,
in the petals
of a face
appearing
in the hallways
of a shattered
reliquary, done
for others gone
to heal
the technicality
that nothing is

a 12 for every
mote that carves
an action
on the trail
that most removes
the palms
from pockets
in the fear
that fire
resembles

13
for memories
that make
a new one
of coyotes
filled with shirts
in fruits
that peel
Before

2 sevens
for the hands
that make a flesh
arrive without
a word
in snows
and settlements
that many know
to ring

a perfect
Zero

•

the 2 an end
for foam
that evenings
plug
to play
the woman
in a letter
that acidic
words
can be

the 2 a faltering
that honey
fits
to tire the green
that wheels
return,
a window
that the trust
will make
to burn
the moth
again

the 2 a tree lined
fruit
that slaughter makes

erasing
what a miniscule
embrace
will see
betrayed
to give
the sound
—a touch

SIETE—A PROXY FOR PHANTOMS

mandan (they send)

like the lost car that a river knows
like the heat of an ointment in pinpoints of breathing
like the unknown western in mountains of tar
like a knot in each word for comfort
like a horse on a face with four hooves
like the knives that a heart squirms into
like the feel that the last day pushes, that a fire paints red
like the shower that a plain divides in snakes
like a frozen torso pining for food
like the ammunition that a pair of wings makes dry
like a shirt that plants seeds under worn out skin
like the clouds of mistakes, pouring through sleep
like the walls that crack open
like a wake in a spin
like the exits of oceans that a salmon knows
like the dust that is written with number
like a trust full of beacons of light
like the negative shade of a fungus
like the promise that a lie gives out
like the pulse of a trap
like the rainbow that cuts off a hand
like a psychic intent full of negative calls
like salt for the season that covers the fields with jail
like the round word that a star pisser pulls

like the plains that a crossed out calendar day will mourn
like the fate of the wrong side of talking
like hills under snow that a letter revolves
like the husky reflections of leeches that writhe
like a sword in Toledo
like the animals growing a vent in a cage
like the sequence of nights dropping straw for a cipher
like the trade in the fair full of cycles and ends
like the cattle that heat all the drains with green grass
like the nipples of outdoor intentions
like a wing on the door that a glass makes arise
like the underground fluid of digitized words
like the ice in a cavern
like a ride through the green light of dying
like the yellowish herd of relational cards
like the face that a wallet becomes
like the wrong line of radios making a rule
like the crust on the last day of hunger
like the rodeo riding the real for a cut
like the cells in the spread of the fall
like an ape for the circle of color
like reflections that turn on a wheel
like the freezer of sweethearts
like a change for the current that makes a return
like the pause on the shore full of rattles
like the oxygen tent making holes in a lung

the face
of friendly fire
is knotted
for a smile

deleted
for a smile
that saves
the executioner

the face
intended
jail, by rocking
through the holes
that fear
the clear blue
family
of dots

the face
resembles
next to nothing
in the network
full of incremental
touches
that a string
intends to limit
by the light

the face
of arctic
evolutions, a hunt
that people came
to read
instead of mapping
all the flights

of sleep
without a sound

the face
of terrible returns
will fade
outside the pouring
crowd
of animal
relation
in the mineral
of wealth

the face
of providence
is making shores
for surfers
in the foam
of magnifying
eyes
that are the opposite
of winter calm

the face
is never there
in each intention
that the worst
reliance
knows to ask
for heat

the face
is after
every opening
that makes
a number
count
for all
of what is good

like a robot that falls and makes good for a switch

like the breasts of a mop that soaks blood

like a magnifying glass for the sun

like the picture of radar in space

like a misery flood on the phone

like electrical laughter that the pointed shake

like enemies held in a double embrace

like extinctions returning

like a handshake of style for the heat

like the flower that bottles a fly for a mouth

like the still dunes of dust on a beautiful girl

like the crack in an oven

like a moon that gets brighter with age

night of attrition

a door
that other icons
wed inside
a field, a straw man
warm
with windows
in the aftermath
of visits, like a worm
is easy
for the time that folds
a wave
under the glass

there
with spheres
that glow,
that accidents
undo, like steel
in a cavernous light—

below

in the distance
that a motion
does for the high rise

scar,
a mirror
through the past

a sentence
comes to others
and dissolves
in sheets
and local scopes

as arrows
that a bow
unveils, a line
that strings
undo, a distance
that the stillness
plows
without a golden
glow—an ash

that yesterdays
uproot
to wear the comb
of rooster calls
around the buzzing
that a phone call
makes in wood,

the answer
severed
by an ocean

that the salt
removes

cicada swarms
unknown
to accidental
letters, servicing
the scientific
drone
deletions
in the hat
that makes recursive
faces

for a motor
as a river thins,
the Float
in cells, a roof
made flat
with travels,
like the wound
that streets remove
and make
into a hole,
a movement,

breath,

a painted surface
like the most
of nullified
intentions,

the withering
that smiles
unveil, to do
what cuts
into the fabric'
of a flesh
that stands
exchanges
in the horror
of a sign

what can surface
for the chair
and circled fingers
as connections
rot
to find an answer
to the mountain
that a moon
resembles

a wave, for birds
is settled down
for sockets
in a motor driven
pulse
that feels like sand

?

what canceled
door can sparkle

for the arms
that days
in other entries
for a city,
a catapulted
flesh
can sing? what

can knives remember
for the ruin
in a spring, a goatherd
for the line of bells
that move
the little bags
of rocks, and mud

in summers
packed
to feel the only
number
that a mass
in patterns
for the error
and an automatic
slough
can steal?

a sun
for digits
ricochets
a swamp

of cattails
on the coast
that writes
a hand

unknown
to zeros
stolen
for the island
in the sleep
that's thick
with thorns

a spoke

artificial tears

the cave is salvaged, it used to weaken all the memories that gave
its sweat to count the shores that couples cut into
for sunlight, as the night that fools a hand that's planted
in the ghost dance of a servile pool that reaches into flesh,
that peels its residence from dirt. when the shower, following
an incantation of a wheel, the dynamited floor under the sea,
becomes its only cause, its only knot tied in connection to the light
of Help—its number notched into the belly of a live-in whale,
its fires below the onion field that pulls the weather by a safe
return that links have after yarns and disassociations,
under trailer tracks and lots of cooking that the sun will show—
give the plant a signal for the molecule that breathes

a centipede of malls and mirror flashes turns a visit to the white
into a double cross, a noontime accident that spills the paint
over a pier, is walking through the shine of ships and bridges that the stranger
pockets in the wall that's cracked and drilled for carving up a line,
a shower of a hologram or placards made to look like windows on a lake,
a trial of calibration and a wedding for what knows to end the word
humiliation plants into the soil of death. windows force the face
of endless eyes in sewers for a smiley that a spiritual will smoke
inside the cake that peels the rain below a bicycle that's plowing
through horizons in the light of each revolver, each intention for the real
that switches its circumference, without a trinity or carcass in the heat
of anthills building time. a hole for others that remember it's a plane

a wreck of all the tables in an alley skirts collapses like
a shore of even plains that stretch to cities on a step
instead of parallel impressions, like the frost and buried key
that turns the lock of cells relieving each of its connections, its additions,
its infinite and referential loss that pulls the eyelids from an otherwise
distasteful silence, like the sideways glance that makes a tool replay
its own beginning, bibles in the igloo that a moon makes more of
for the underlying sentence in a tumor of enlightenment and grace. you
will end in sovereign pulses by the opening that stays outside
the only visit that a net of stillness, a crowd of incubational reversals
does what other broken angles in the bed of links can see. an apple
that the serial can say begins, with images of rain and flattened skies

will move inside the frost that beacons pamphlets full of lamps
through headless raids that pile a blessing for a trace of feet that lead
a child to chains. its juice, like Mars and moons projecting in a Latin
accent, for the letters that recorders fossilize in empty diners, in
the symbol that can never be alone. a door that music sends to heal
the sentence growing from a tongue that turns, a vast retarded wilderness
a player fills to bend her limbs to quiver with a lozenge that the loss
of second languages becomes. the anger of a tree that feels its need
is here to stand among the birds that know the answer inside seeds that never
fall, inside the flattened out responses that renew a trade,
shed all its skin, for good, for rains that settle toggled eyes, a radio
that makes a funny form of whipping, starchy yeses that belong to cells.

the pier that makes a weekend feed its starving fish just once
makes calls erasing all caresses, all the openings that fool the mouth
into believing that a road is made of ice in winter, in the heat
the road is made to cut into the living of a trade before a jungle
in the eyes of one that moves in rain to track *mamones*, in the plains
that predators with wings make into pathways for an Easter

under prisons in the West. what can die alone can live in two,
in work abscessing plays that quake an obligation for a time,
to place one's head inside the vice of conduct, rattling the gates
for light to come inside desertions, in the pleasant code of every
mole that lines itself behind the double axe of sleep, the fleeting
glimpse of sorry camps, still, another bale of straw makes home

the dust of welcome, dust of others, dust of disconnected mouths
before a storm of tiny clouds makes hands spread out and give
a bus its early morning freeze, its church yard in the gaze of distances,
held in hands for memories of docile convicts in a room that others
shrink to be themselves. this place is what the light reveals, a piston
smeared with grease to open up the sound inside a promise, more
than letters can repel to be the warmth that places all the kisses
of an afterlife inside the weaker image in the square that angles its
replies. a bag to give the color its incision, underground
deterrence that a signal for connection floods for others, for the crowd
that feeds on glass for cleaner thoughts, and feelings in the vein
along the limbs of trees and older places in the south around a wheel.

it borrows each contusion, each pathology to make a she an it a he
for credit, for the salivating vibe that makes a shelter out of scabs
and makes a living for the poor in water that the flag
fills with a thousand treasures, a mansion in the placid field
protected by the guards of wooded pleats, standing tall and clean
and still, ready for the onslaught of a cause that's just and trading
for the wound that never was so big that screens could fit the suffering
to make big tickets feel like they were kind. so kind that even poetry
would make its way into impoverished people that were other
like scores of spines that stood around the wealth that one day
stood around the rows of stacks that it could not read into, like the feelings
that a porch or midnight round of trash picking could sink into an ass

of walking through the generosity and understanding of the few.
make a statue for the wood that mothers mourn, the still birth
that begins instead inside me, not a rumor that is crowded
wrapped around an answer full of gravel in the grave that friendship
steals to wear the entrance of a masked cathedral, sharpening
the knives that slaughter words. a skeletal reminder in reflections,
a ring from telephones that cut into the lungs of loam and planted
maps that grow into the longest day, the line of enemy connections,
like a grovel in the season of a better deal—more error for the truth,
the colors of a racetrack in the blue reply of starlight, in the stolen
log, an argument that mountains and the ash that covers first an eye,
then sound and coastal villages along the arms, a listening of wet

dimensions for a hole and totem that an empty blow up doll
will circle with its lips. the toggle driven signal of a lover,
in the box of never saying what will function for the light,
what the numeral decides outside an ocean in the season
of the insect burrowing into the hummingbird that knows
the nectar of the end of maps, in drenching, accidental
peeled off skin, a greeting from the tiny ancient wheel,
a million hands cut down to make the presence of a knot
grow through, without a root among the flowers, fissions
for the stalker that a towel wraps into cages, while the count
makes traps come in. plead again without a sound,
moving what a state of polygons would write for truth,

for opposite remarks inside the weather of the 13 other
solar clouds, and planet chains that light will make
more solid, like the earth. an underlined regurgitation
for the younger shoots inside lagoons and blackened
pools of seeing, for the scrape that settles visits,
for an iron that makes the arms more steady, more like

river reeds that pour the sand into a swamp and serve
its alibis for colder feet to lessen in long lines
of patterns for the ground and sky that rubs itself
on landmarks for the iron of seeing,
for the endless travels in a cell. what will migrate
under pollen, will return with cities in a circle

and with particles that fill the eyes with movement,
give a hand another road to carry carcasses
in early morning canyons swarming with the eagle
of a cripple, singing with the bones that fill policemen
with the taxi cabs of longing, in the shower of a curse,
on shores that break the blooms of camps
along the wrestling trees of computation,
in the downtime of a warning, in the error
that will leave you twice alone. keep the beeping light
on painted torsos in the river that the lost become,
and shovel out the corn that turns into the day
when snakes become the image of beginnings, and tongues

renumber all the fields of other countries, in the end
there is a channel to remind the dead that one day they will be
as one is two, as next to nothing, and two as three to wake
with four as seven, eight in riding through the war. place
the search of engines in the planet of a winter that the sea
will fade into, unknown to all the rodeos that make a visit
like the century that comes without a face, a target, all
the bodies gone to make the shame relieve its own reflection
from the map that leaves the forest for the light and carves
the fat from fabrics that the softened age of unborn witness
will report, and start the horses that will ride for absence,
for the nature that a split inside the word will plant, to give

the shiny one

showers here
import the heat
in caverns

quiet, electric
distant throats

the signs connect
a page
in crystalline
interiors,
in warmed up
thorny wires

a motor saddled man
makes voices
sound outside
the air. what he does
is in a space
in two, on a bed
with wooden pillows
for the news. a cage
in video, a snuff—
intentions
of a hungry ghost.

fuses
that a public
runs into
make fronts
for feet
in networked
stars along the bottoms
of a trial. boxes
make the ceiling
big,

a feast
intends
like light
the willow wears
a plastic skin
for cause,
the radio
delivers
in the rain
that put together nights
belong to heated
shores

the lake
is carved
in lightning
for the morning
that a dragon fly
makes sleep
move into waves

the price
of people
in the plastic shoot
turns fall
for space,
a mobile
that the presence
of a mood
of walls
makes solid
for a turn

they run a camp
to make the desert
call for bridges,
shots of time
around casinos
in the gate
that feeds the statue
with a bird,
a stick,
the heat
that floods a double
on a train
arrives, without
a trail

countless colors
for a border
integrated kiss, cut off
the store

that planets
green with distances
in aching
ovals, all
arriving west
to graft
in clicks
the morning
pulls
the herd
of menaces

it's better lost
and deadened
in the aftermath
of sentimental
hallways
full of moving
floors
along the personal
discovery of laws
that shape
a palm, the net
of goggles
made of stone
to see the ruins
of the truly gone

i make a mouth
more empty
for the fish

that hook
into the words
that float, mud
can speak the other
name that cracks
the ball,
planted
on a ladder
that will break

the digit splays
in bundles
in a mouth,
a television
momentarily
invisible,
outside
along the acres
of initializing
nights, together
on the plank
that writing
puts into
a home

its memory
is viral, and releases,
written in
to steal
a wooden idol
for defections

that belong
to accidents
for kites that leave
and falling knives
that hide
within a breath

the ride that seven makes

a run
at making sevens
in the morning, on the wall
a bird
and others
mark the basement
yesterday
for trading
for a face
in quarries
under heat.

a ball of light

appears at night

inside my sleep.

a hill, a move
as worms deliver—in the fertile
casket
that a function
torn to shreds
will make alone, outside
a seer
by the bridge
a meeting
for the lost

that cakes
the arrows, on
the front
of less
than flesh. Word—
a voice
is plowed
into a downward
slope, an ache
in chalk

that feet
resemble,
on the other side
of twins, the rest
that evening
veils
to riders when
there is none
as you wrote

gone, for good
and gone
for beauty.

ugliness

can breathe

and equal all
the truth
that carves
your face. doesn't it

resemble you?

for i
for r

for one that ends

for every voice

for maggots in the shade,

for sleep at random in the rain

more for winter
in the morning
that a system sees

once forgiven
empty cells
the spinning light
extinguishes

a breath
the rope
is evening—
steps from exits
call
a shiver—
sheets of ice in giving
for commands

one that empties
never sees
the count

                    of one together,
                    one before

knots that make
a winter start
are piled
in planks
of shriveled stars

the end of trials
makes blood
go still

the truth
of animals
arrives

          to wake the shards in will
          and link the seasons,
          rot for moons
          to walk the cells—not any

                              one.

as wrong a name
is given
to the door, the empty
eyes that spin
through ceilings,
in the aftermath
of frozen solid
seals,
a memory

of dolls that mark a room
with entrails
by the double exit
that a trial
becomes, for farmers
in the pathways
of a blackened fruit
the crater goes together
with a fuzzy lock
in services, Antarctic
lights that fuel
a knot inside, the rest
beside a channel
for the war
that clips a feeble
rain, without
your warmth
in cylinders
and glass
that hates the vessel
in a space
that cracks

that leaves the warmth
and plants
the heaving target
of an end

the way across
a voice

the flash

the intent of your resemblances, like the older part of continents,
is a whirlpool full of limbs,
is a light around the body of the fully formed, is broken
through the sky that's black and swollen
planting into networks what a signal
of the plains of velvet under rain filled boxes in the sky
makes still. swollen tongues split roads within themselves
to link an object to the better part of things
forgotten
by the bound and braided
puncturing
that pours a weaker definition of a self, to magnify
a nature's full, identical, and ending
pieces put together
for anemones. a mapping floats the number four
and draws through endless slashes
smaller countries in the window of the longest light. knots
undone inside send coasts an equal, in the middle
of a neck that otherwise
can never carry
what the clouds that burn inside a hutch
wrap in themselves, to bury the allegiance
of a god installing a connection full of emptiness
and shot into the sand. a comet that a place before the snow
became, the priceless strip of flesh that mines into itself
a voice, a bird without a feather in the palms of infants

as a sign, comes down and makes the seeing end. a misery
in towers made of Arab
resolutions, a run initialized
for more than chance,
a weave that powers off, a ridicule that bonfires hold
up to the night, is standing for the pond
that ice reflects under a swarm
of the unknown. a freezing rain cuts down circumferences
of circles that betray
perfections in the nature
of the timeless reason that a fool has
to arrive in chains. the chains that make a word
resemble its incisions
in a face that never had an opening, the hole
that life in everyday installments
digs into a passing
of the steps of always meaning to become. duration
is a sentence and an end
of arrows on the screens that make the world
believe in splashing out the sun.

the tiny dots i spit into my hands
without a language that a meal, inside the light, returns
rewrites the line that's written, that i die
without a trace in any of the countries that you claim
a mother, as a sister full of glass
releases the assignment that machines
revolve around, in knotting the ascent of anchors
in the screens that mark your land
with needles, for the string
that strips the welcome from the angry visits
to the single aim that likens an emergence

of a spanish word in hooded trials, a better law
than what a person in the warmth of tunnels,
on the feet that never knew the cold, can see. do the arrivals
of a song delay, in rows and rows of fronted tics
hiding the ingredients that poison what you swallow?
with an apron for the bloody mouth
rivers mark inside the neighborhood, a simple
deal that magnifies the slide in front of me
the throbbing ice inside my skull
keeps the patrons from the newly formed
contagions flood the lockers full of jumping
out of pressing through the word. a color
for the answer of a fraction of a float, the warning
in a freeze
of stairwells
in the necks of animals with daisies
on the hill
that bleats, a latin carcass
feeds the cage. the porcelain betrays the prayers
at noon,
the better part of changing
for the accent that the husk of accidents
revolves around the winter
in the get together that a darkness
turns to negatives
like phrases that a river holds
for crossing,
for disease. a radio makes lesser
what the mathematics of a robot
cures for sleep, for longish visits to the past
delivered in magnetic vesicles and cannabis
for screeching like a feather held outside the air,

a stretch that makes a ride that twists, a hive
that's full of bees, and rain. the weaker plush allows
a visit to the friend that hides a knife that's unpredictable, well known
to the confections of a rodeo, the newer lasso
a painter shows to keep
the magnified release of pilfering
the room that's sinking, full of sand, that disappears.

the lines and marks in snow banks are erased
like summers found
by swimming, by the fish that stole
the eyes and arms from visitors
that make their home inside reflections, in the wings
that cut into the permanence and petrified
intention, a car that's full of music for the lost
will claim to give a word
for parched and stitched relations
of the good inside the less than bought. what can claim,
or who can outline for a mute, the mounds
that fill a stadium with midnight visits to a parking lot
for recitation and a view?
as generosity remembers, as the law that heritage
will light the stars to sparkle on the tops of trees,
and names that echo
for the nipples
sending signals to the other worlds
and feverishly delivering
a rancid milk of desperation
to the plants. the names that count the heat as their resourceful
guide through trees that mark the wind
with scents, repair
the predators that play outside the safety and the balance

of the pools of sweat
that fell, with athletes and ones that lost, they represent
releases in the carriage house
alleys lead into
for pockets full of keys
that have no place to make into a refuge or a hole.

they were seasons
when the picture
was a clearer view
of night as day, inside
the volume
of a wall

they were younger visits
for the aisles
that later filled with trains
and aching light
within a blood loss
that the dead become

a provocation
of a satellite
moves outside
a trailer
full of cooking
and the sleep
of endless
repetition

a weapon and a fuse
will make a word

as snow mounds like beginnings
stay the same as any cloud

tandem

the wake before the open half of creaking sounds
makes many of the drops that color each horizon,
planted in a trap with springs, a newer
shower in the veins that travel in a sharpened
match that's made for mornings that will run. a poison

valley that a schoolboy carves into a number, floods
equations that the moisture in a word will float
beside each quarry, in the diver that a prehistoric
predator remains inside, to weaken in the tar. a wall
that fleas remind the crystallizing harpist on a wave

believes and walks beside a conversation that the steel
for stiff instruction wades without the newly born,
the boat that means its triangle is crowded, for a hand
in measurements that flock to rain the cattle's wood
to seals and networked crones inside a better visit

for a rule. a miser and a mystery can run outside
each frothing cold without its only shower in the snow, its one
together with a mine, within magnetic moons that cross
the promises in each of its intentional receivers, windy
camps filled full with intersections and a view. choose

the mountain hollowed out into volcanoes, highways
split, received, to warn the heat that settles on the floor
grown out from our dismembered moon, the settlement

that promises will stagger in the evening of a mark
in showers that a particle in each of the deliveries of one

of the installments of another life can make to stand
in open sightings for the keyed in explanation, for the way
that lips improve upon a square. the razing house that makes
another cave into a safe, a winter cut into for roots
of knotted up relations that a people plant to make a friend

of rupture, in the backward crescent fusing the intention
for a link, a pan, a service on its rainy mornings spent
beside the incantation of a war, a plastic wrap revealed
to wear the down in flying insects, like the quiet flight
of owls. remember that the weekend full of murders

can equate itself with noonday visits by a desert
growing through the magnified intention of a breath,
deceived and planted with a heart, a parallel envisioning
a corky shame will aim to see. shoveled out
of youngish visits in a face reflected on, a tied in two

reconnaissance that infinite relations crowd inside
for petty streets to shine away with rain, absorb
the fattened insurrection that a song divides
to see the wound that other servants make the protocol
implant a kindness as a weapon for the naked in a pool

of two's intent, the hard and metal guides that flood
a life that's weak and aimed at making food of spineless
caravans and marches through the bowl that's full
of residential perforations. a canister that spins around
and marks the next in line to die, promises a day

will never be as full as night, as empty as the hands
that soldiers carve themselves to listen, to the fire that peels
against the signals that a river full of doubt rehearses for the answer
that a people in the snow assemble for the overhaul
a center wants to crash. a viral, still foundation that a flaw

resembles, starts with following the technical delivery of holes
and gleaming cuts that several gowns and empty stalls
resend their focuses and links for raw encounters, for the bear
that once intended negative replies for light. make the seed
a running coat that, legless, can invent a shower in a virtual

relation for the once in sequence, once the followed, its second
apparition through the body of a wordless stance. solid indiscretions,
like direction, can define identity for groups that negatives
repair, a fallen log inside extinguished friends that wilderness
remakes into for longing, for the sewer that a memory, a blue

replacement for the promise of an ended name, removes. a name
that people wash into for corners cut outside the sound
that it might be, a magnet in the heart that he becomes, nothing
settled in the carriers that sold the only time intended
for the arrogant and calm. what do people in their pedestals

and calcified regurgitations do for them that settle
for a horse, a window, newer standards that communications
fold into for energy. a run that fakes the bird that promises
a view to stop inside a car, a winnowed plain that stiffs
vocabularies in a manager, and in a heart concatenated,

salivating on the door. you, grower of a pain that folds into
itself, sewer of the laughter that a tiny ball can see
to bounce us through the light, a highway

less than water in its easy flight through desperation,
like the people that a purity in one resolve can make to ratify

a simple course, the racetrack full of fuzzy fire, can go away
and die into the particle that rattles, for the nest of slowed
down tigers that the underground intent of limbless
rulers, like the maggot under crowns, the season
that correction, like a bomb that knew that he was called

a death for others, for the sleeping cow that tumbles
through a winter in return. fail, inside a segmentation full
of baubles, in the orient that flowers through the expiration
full of rested eels. one won't ever have to reach, to be a flame
of evil, in the wads that fever places for a twice together

breathing in the dark. a network integrated for the shower
in a lifeline for the willing, pink and orange in the sky, in cracks
that break a bottle in affection, in the tracks,
a roving hunter sends to you her plans, a wooden desk
is leveled, with water in the fuel of little bombs. magnetic

clips inside the rib cage of the recently forgotten, push
out pointers for the hanging plant that never knew
the love that shrank and battled its demise, to stiffen
in the halter of a flesh filled rain, carved by a remission
of the cancer of the good. networks for the radios

that cause a democratic hash to beacon—it's alive
with welts that make a criminal a stretched out limb,
a salvaging of this, your twice together goat, make
the rain its own, its weary system full of all
the crowded intersections, all the coins that one day

flag the truth and give out steady farms for ounces
full of heat and cowardice. a strong relation to the weak
can give you countries many more than friends,
when equilateral intent refuses its primordial
report for tropics in the palms of tiny plants. the cost

of rackets cut into for visits to the family and openings
that fewer words can see through, for a bag that sells
the breathing rites to any wanderer that settles
in the plain, enforcing an amendment to agreements
that the steady flow of friendly shores can make to end

the sun in shriveled up replies, for solitude that's loud
with other games, in films that write a welcome
for their own impending knives that sit, a freezer full of magic
lambs—a dozen birds that fill the air with arrows
watching horses breathe. the steps into the night that follow

go again presenting time, and come again to rest in resignations
full of silent clouds that many walk to give the light
its nails. a crowd that pulls the star from outer reaches
in the penitent and hiding, cuts the winter from the agonizing
spring. a sheet of blue can shiver off the visit to a cliff

and promise that the circuit on the forehead of the newly gone
will place a field, the causeway, other parties in the sand
and make its unknown lips drop through the pearls
and land into beginnings full of cattails, in the visit
that will feed the wilderness its vain attention to the fern

ISTHMUS

still quiet

still quiet, a letter falls to break the earth. a spark
diffuses, like the fog on a clear day, the clear day
under clouds, for seeing. for the clear day under a single cloud, under continents

it's impossible to draw a line between the petals, the droplets in the air
like frogs, like the traveling earth
that a hand undoes inside the longest call, in the sewer, with a frog

graffiti marks on an "at home" side. count out that a sign slows
magnetic yarns, as cause—
that the dead mark. i know the wall as exits, for singing

the wall is gone—says the digit, walking, breathing to mark
the spring with white roses
in the dark. a link between miniatures, no longer difficult

i let go of the hot air balloon in the story, an accident
plows through the heat
as the summer makes sounds inside the still balloon

the stories of the sign are gone, as the wound saddles
to say why
an icicle falls. the stitched exit that a mind makes, like space

i see the days in each palm, an island calls
to the worn horizons, the view is
not gone. and is not anywhere that a knot settles into, light extinguishes

questions sprout by the bridge, and only for the bridge
as the cold
moves forward, sprawling out from a wooden shell, to nowhere

the afterimage of a satellite, an entrance embalmed by prehistory
that negations play to, to see
on the northern side of the river that brings on the afterimage of a satellite

the radio that a planet buries together with darkness, the radio done
to hear a solitary vowel
in the integration that stars become before dying, in the radio transmission

a disease that the social equate with intention, in the abandonment
of a spherical cloud
that the disease calls itself, the disease of name and witness

penetrates the olive grove, the sweat run wires that swap the skies
to page a view
a view that penetrates a black olive with what is seen, surrounded, on the ground

with a hand to hand reflection, the stolen time that a city warms
in winter
with a park that moves with murmurs, that insists and contains the snow

a time that stalls, in the violent mind of a pacifist
is what the image says
in a fixedness and sudden intersection that pours out light

the unsolved resistance that makes enemies of the intangible
nears itself at every moment
to release the cities in a pulsing magnetic attraction

the extra sounds in a song that explode the circle between persons
is made to last
in the meal among strangers and a song that makes circles

the revolver that marks up the spiders in an anasazi ruin
remains at the same time
as the time that is gone, and is still, and is not a target

a lily marks the side of the face that remembers, that it steals
that the mother undoes
in herself, in the passion of white that a lily mourns

in the answer is a road that ends, a road that intersections extend
to surface in the only disease
that a face ever has, as denial will not stop the edges of incision

if symbols line up to the angry beggars, for snow, for the apparition's
activity that dissolves in the war's networks
and the fame that an earthy innocence will die for returns as loss

the underside of a river is full of birds in Colorado
and their diamonds
are scattered in the salt mines that my eyes run into

the forest of lesser known music, like the city
is reported to be continually heard
like the light in the sea of the poles and arrivals, as it dies

a tape in the winter worn stories, the unknown disaster
that cannot write
is here in the wind, it motions the scars on the moon

a fever that the sand intends, its nuptial breath
delivered, like an egg
in the town that a hand destroys, and begins to know, is still

the conversation lasts for many mountains, as its trails are burned
and its trees are bent down
to make the furrows and rainbows that smother the fields

a mother is like the conic shells that make sounds
in the morning, for teeth
that a forest forgets, as she always occludes the light, and plants in the dark

extraterrestrial information technology begins here. the soft soil
that waiting makes outside
itself, folds another echo in a word, a single point in the sky that breaks

there's a shed skin on the plains that paints marks in a cave, the only weapon
that a stalled hatred, the missing resemblance
to the flesh eaten family, to the nocturnal hangman that a child stares at, is here

the man that followed me at night, that returns again as in sorcery
was there when a vision began
and returns to see the insects swarm with their recognition of my mouth

to speak in a way that cuts light and time into each sound, like the dance
between the desert and the sea
that the sacrifice of arms negates, that a cripple holds on to for sustenance

even an exception in the word, the shelter that never warms,
the alone time without a return
that the negation of meaning will not end, appears as a crack in the ground

the resolution of justice, that the wronged will not say, that the life
of escape
where no relation exists, that is the start of vision, with exits in both eyes, begins

to live each moment as if forever invisible, the lack of time that brings
true life
to the unwanted, a wound breaking open like a field of stars, circulates

i have a background in numbers, like the body forms that fill the square
in the halting gate that a counter locks
to wear down the gas pumps at the service station, to see more palms erase

the increase in the angle at which sunlight pours in through the endless airport
cuts through the neighborhood and undoes
the field full of tremors and the ground swelling with cicada songs

the impoverished is saddled with gold, the gleaming report that an island heats
moves into the tender sac
that a body fills, streams in the forest make accents in the middle of a white room

a cross for the forgotten friends that return and tie up the affable prisoner
with winter the skin is sold
as anyone enters your private reserve, your information palace

without a center, the canyon that settles each emotion, to ring
the mastery of idleness and shame
keep the desert on the trail of clouds and make a tunnel a child's dream

there is only one way to be dead in the face of employment, and to see
the incubations
that a cradle follows on the absolute and solid joy of blind lies and desperate safety

a broken trade

you are folded
and the water
runs
into the floor

these surfaces
remove, an action
a word
intends
for cells, like soap
your horns
push through

or the woodland
buried
in each arm,

the unintentional
increase of coins
in tiny trains,

a track makes hands
an isthmus
with a torso
in the unannounced

reprieve
the sand once more,

to hear

to open

in dissecting tables
a swell,
a smile,
a hanging,
from the eye,
a mountain
in a range
of rounded plastics
thin themselves
into the dust

of points
and swell to heat
a circulating
stack of twins
in infinitely
arriving coasts,
and moves
beside a hungry
host, a cut

that sends you
parallel
with leather counts,

the face
winters
fear
for pushing out
the snow

beside the fire
it frames
a hand
with numbers
and the moist
delivery
of death

you
that smallish spines
will stand, a place
without the news
in dots
track kindnesses
an unknown ice
returns, to hands,

to turning visits
for the endless lie
a vision grows

into a mound
of loam and tender
clots
inside

an oily
loss
of seeing chains

when there's a question
for the zero
a swelling
by the mouth
puts out,

a pus filled globe
in buds
increasing
for the world to save
itself, like caves
in safe
electrocutions:

a vow,
a predator,
a leech
can be—as one

as if it is assigned
to siblings, in the grid
it lights an island
through a weave
inside the moon, explosions
in the sky
that elements
can bear, a sound

bleeds
and gives to counters
to believe, it said
that this was one
around the time
their places roam

the fields are soaked
with life negating moss

and rid
of ties to fingers
in the screen
that never dies. equating
with a deafness
in the swirl that gives
its time to wind away
the spheres of stone
are hidden

when a fern
will radiate
for lips
in steel
that calls
a wound
it bleeds
escape

and pleads
with its intention, his, and

its and hers, and seeming
to the stack
the many sticks
are put together
like the type of empty
roads
carry you
to circle
in the dark

mobile seeds
will rest
and split
the light
of rain

random lake

in the winter a winter song, the dead remove, they see, the execution
of the middle, the pouring through of abandoned shelters
and a past is planted to seek out an opening, an end
a city dissolves in, an accident removed from the appearance of white space,
all gifts, all the falling and false tremors
a heart in its stretchy sail, the threat snowballs, growing speed
outside, in the morning's
neck, its outer planet, a room
with people soaked in gas, remain, return, and catch the dark
beads, the injured, stiff with poses, will intend, for warmth.

una fijeza de palmas

the easter bonnet, the alley in its soap and foils, an enormous
tentacle and flower hid face weeps, along
a flood of small greetings, a crab coldness feeds into for foam
and mystifying waves, as hives, as billboards on a hill,
beloved
wheels. the open source
runs a cavity with extra rocks and ports,
the ashes and the horse alone with steel, intends
a bucket for the color, a number for the song, a square
for integers and calming wars, they know the sentence of the salt in ending
waves, as fallow
on the track and picture cut for arrows, as a time in sheets
to hang the fields
in ancient cups of farmer framing lies (the cold).

everyday, two days, one lost to the stationary ambulances, in a sentence
the animals can see
for sale, for the aim that settles packets, forgotten,
a single blade of grass vacated, always, in the oceans
meaning moves to end
the reddened signals like a searing highway
under each return, missing roots a wind makes dry
fields, delivery
of the picture filled with a single eye.

once, in once, there is once together by noon
on the green tablet, the sled
scores, and every sun, the heat of an aisle, twisted for a word,
stays, stalls, and increases the empty tub
a gather of air, the blood, the pools filled with city ice
and a question, the look wood remains, to press
the fields floating on fire
and lesser known intentions, to separate with warnings.

a network begins and ends with ownership, the switching state
of countries, an ancient wall
the sand weaves into, for a storm, in a canary's song
a pearl grows with death
for an ocean in flames, protections
and race hatred, a hat makes
for a peaceful sun
burns. letters fade into the wall, and the basement
hears her willows, and the night
bleed, a child, fading, in the ash,
breathes a holy fuel.

you burn well on the altar made of shells, and on the roof
a promise, the anchorage
and handshakes
poured for memories of love, it's only time,
and the opposite
of time. cake
for the rabid mark and metal
cause, the wind, the open face
a friend knots up for entrances, a lineage
for actions, snow fills the quake
with Easter, tortured smiles
and bulging skin that memory records, slowly, from afar.

see, the enormous egg, rolls, ever   for the noonday pause
and a slow shine,
falsettos born along the shorelines a needle
skewers, a shell, the light
a castle fading
microscopic aims arranged for espionage
in murders
for the indices, a room filled to the top with boxes and equations,
a song overflows with the invisible
wounds, and endless visits
the pasture
ready, for the slash and burn
comes for night   is still

déjame sin gente

my father
was a snake

my mother
was a cockroach

i love them both
as the darkness

loves each side
of the night sky

mis canciones
son las islas
en los ojos
de los muertos

when i see the side
of the word
on your side, the side
speaking, the side
warm, the day equates
with feathers
and a new tropical
extinction, by the place
full of birds
the opening, the related
star
does not end, does not speak, does not ask
what the ashes do in the fire
by the shore, the midnight hurt
that a bed
in its spirals, the floor still
in the dark, the answer
puts out

by secretive connections,
is here, is the sound
a mother makes
when she is the end
of all words,
and has long ago passed
the dog

good company
for a face
in a whine
of attacks

how does one force
the mountain,
the trees,
the hatred
born
that runs aground,
into the everyday,
the link by link
makes ready
for a cell, how does the ache
white walls excite
make the call
answers, the request
for living
that a paper plane
bombs
outside the cavities
that fill with seasons
end?

universal indians

(after Albert Ayler)

i unravel the song in the knots in the chest of the broken
with emergencies planting a network of islands in heat
and fissions that fuel all the work in the dust of the land
of the burning and shadowy icons

a grid in the forest of smaller intentions, the group full of eyes
an exit prevents, like the knowledge that time does not turn
for a son that the poison rejects, in the eastern most prison
chickens defend, is the map for a face

the promise the houses on fire will turn into ash and mark up the bodies
of numberless chants and the holes that the ointment repeats
and the kiss that a weather makes local for fire in the globular
ghost, will discover the islands that hearing makes still

and the video ward in the prayers of a desperate ending, in the service
that feeds with mirages a scar that the healing arranges with flowers
for unity flooding the roots in eruptions
and mind, makes the wind carve a word in the space of a skull

for the people capital kills, and relation for dirt in the hands of the mourners
a heat in the pylons glowing at night, the traffic is swelling
to hear in the rain what the planets can visit for nothing
and the seasons can shred

in a pendulum riding the time for the service of other reports, in a viewer
it sparkles the call of a suicide door for the entrance to magnify

lines in the skin that a reader relates to a dwelling, oils in the sleep
of a drowning resource for the honey

in a wooden retry, in the visit it hears in the town full of headless rehearsals
and monuments catching the whole full of islands and entries for numbers
hobble the kites in the storms of a hole in the face of the person that welcomes
the most in a skin for the country that handles a zero

for ashes and lakes in the sewer it binds with addresses and makes the initial
a window for light in the grave of a welcoming signal, a link
in the giant it hears with the hay bail what hummingbirds visit for summer
with tremors as heartfelt releases and boats in the death of intention

as buckets and signs in the street of a miserable lecture for tacks that the swollen
resemble and harvest for jackets and silos in skies
for voltage and canine releases all over the mace that a city collects
and makes comfortable captures as endless extinguishing corpses

forever resembling falseness and wilderness emptied of color and full of the fur
a series of games in the handoff that steals for a rhythm
and doesn't remember, and doesn't resemble the triplicate answer
of quartz and abandoned resources, that is wound in a cradle

and never returns, and rehearses each day for the last day of knowing
for standing and welcoming words in our foreheads
with carnivals flattened and dressed for the tarry mistake
a history marks in the hand of the lost in the ground

without the ascension a friendship impregnates with circles
all over the rattle that sinks with the fish that a miniscule run
for the season that stretches the end of the day for a pulse
and makes a whole species deliver survival

in earthquakes that end the foundations of corporate hugs
for personal letters combining the murder for smiles full of sand
in the quicksand that hovers with ointments along the related
contusions that fuel the pronounceable keys

that intend the collection of deaths, the increasing internal
dissections that fold in the spring time with corpses
arranged for the picnic with countable kisses and ruins
in songs, that executive sabers erase

the hurt of a gaze of affection, in separate ovens they cure
with the owls that a predator sees and relieves in the dark
the ice melts away and moves branches through landscapes
sinking the home of a neuter for segments in storage for others

with a plane for the sentences ending the mother, the father,
the son for a country that never existed, a newborn announcement
makes the attention for networks carve into the skin and the skull
a single word sounding the end of a knot, for the knife,

for a flower related to engines and number, the root of a tumor
inside the arrangement of eyes and the presence of nectar
in blood and the scab of a newer recession, the bomb full of traffic
and walking through fields in the skeletal darkness

fills the replenishing stream full of birds and the sorrow
inside an inflated remission, the sight of a network that hangs with a heart
full of answers and letters and endless uploading, the word that the false
makes a morning and sundown makes quick with caresses

and windows do not fill the skin with a sun, or the night with the moonless
resemblances poured through the light that a distant return, a cattail

that sings with the marshes and holds all the tar that the glaciers inside
will remember, will move with the down that a simple attention dissolves

under stress and the promise that livestock and stealing remain
for otherwise stable recursive amends, and the forest that burns
in the heart of a mountain it stands and comes down
on the man that a network repairs

without sounds and the nourishment meant to be human, the frost
of metallic derision, the kinship that towns far away make with envy
and lust, on the trail of a vulnerable street that's on fire
in the city that tells with its signs what a hand will not hold

•

a snow bound train, an owl in its heated attention, with markers
ruins the words of a ghost and the hands that are lost for the people
all over the mountains, in each of the radios building the ashes
piled on exchanges of nets and a gift for the circle of mouths, makes it easy

for windows that break and make trails in the fate of a wilderness calling
the engines of presence, the sticker that covers the walls of return
with the names of the lost and the forever gone, the roads filled with deer
and a sign that a dance will repair what the city renames

with each of the animals frozen and running the snow down the peaks
of a crystal, and tearing the bodies of sacrifice, not any that made what they
wanted, not any that knew that the street would not end, for each of the bats
in the nighttime that's filled with the oil of the pores in a broken down skin

without the announcements that people remember, the rest of the shackles
that pounce on the arms and the want of a number, a season
renewed and released by the armies that never stay still, that sell
what the wheels of their deserts might sing—

louder than horns, a frown on the child and the balls in a game
of the rules of your time, of the isthmus that saddles the places that age
with negligent cops and a promise that no one will know what the smile
on the ground will devour, then visits to planets

meet with the option of throwing the water all over the stars
and filling the rivers with claws, and the state that an accident says will record
what a séance with empty releases will toggle
on each of the maps that the new world intends, will not settle

as once was the shattered reflection that snakes will remember in scales
in aisles that are swelling with corn, in the raft
a single revision, multiplies rooms and the planet
and fills the alarms with a nectar that bleeds with recursions

and that place the compressions of answers and lakes in the wheel
of a tumor that builds the alignments with straw and connections
erasing the line from within the recession and turning the skeletal
rainbows that fill in the cave of a neutral engagement

with crashes and fire and the lords of a fallout that heals
the attention with shrinking incisions and weaker relations
to soil and the bird that the noontime will follow with breath
and a forest of wandering camels

alone with a visit and under the tables that gleam and pronounce
what a canyon fills with a tear
and with faces come down
and in ointments catch flies, in the sound

the man who ate himself

the easter bonnet
and a bruise,
a highway mask
and trees
by mirrors
and a chance, the sea
makes eyes
for waves that end
the broken wings
and bells, it sits
for fruit
from gifts
in drains
that empty continents,
and fuel,
numberless, a drop
in bodies held
by water, flying
pushes tearful
knots,
endless,
soft with heat
and pain

the iceberg
count, a view
a season cuts
for trade in tender
strings, the frozen
guide by posses
in a river
and lost cages,
still and needing
water cannons
forests darken
wrecks, the snow
a choiceless
place, a range
of hearing, in its
calculation, window
grace, the balance
that a sound with its
recognizance, its letter
even, by the knees
and walking
spots of blood
in snow
each slot
the quiet
early morning
sees, is

a fallow place
that never rises
with the fields

of straw mounds
in horizons, a manikin
the country floods, the fuse
alignments
of the pores
in stretched out circles
for the thaw
that never tracks
arenas, in the sand
that misses
a replacement
as a trailer
gone to peel
the steeples
by the dogs
that sound
the alleys
in the snow, arrives. each
of the intentions
for the bark
a nighttime visit
by the group
steals lilies
for the white
and heals
a reddish wound
is covered up
with skin
like fruit, to roll
the road
that ends

a piece of lettered
gauze, on limbs
the dust
that settles for the stories
in attachments
all the saddles
circulate
a floor that breaks
for each of the revolving
each of the entombed
and all the pull
that moons relay
in salt and greenish
islands full of first
and second
times to one,
starts, and pierces
graves, a totem
for the seal
that magnifies the exits
under squares
and fleshy canyons,
a harvest
for the hornet—
a hidden
hibernation, for the sun
and freezing
loss, the patter
of a punctured word
and all the carving
temples that machines

remember, for the spring
that means a house
the size of ants and flags
and speed alone
along the coasts
becomes

i mean the cages, in a mall
the messages the new
secretions, for a family
that's stuffed with tar
and hijacks, cold—
a forest
in the empty cave
its threaded news
and ice, gravel
gone to wear away
the numberless
and quaking tubs
a messenger, the side
of here, the newer
accident, the light
an answer gives, given
making words
and circles
shaking ferns
the thieves
in houses, fire
is gone, to sleep
announcements
come, the standard

cause and bloom and cash
a pregnancy, the place
keeps number
here to make an ocean
in embraces
and warm
tents

binarius

an iceberg in a vent surrounds the spine
with ankles down the hills, a fall
with roots in the between, peels the skeletal
intention of a face

a shout floods quicksand in the winter
a memory of lexical revisions, snow on top of floating
torsos. a feed quickens letters in the wrong
relinquishing, an answer—

the peace of angry visitors connecting to the moon
with frozen tongues make choirs
shout out the anthems in the stars that others hang
for still absorptions, and the skies

the fashion of a smile, filled with coal and shining
nights, a queue aligns the sores and horses
meant to drive away the visitors and code. gone
to finish each of the projected souls, come

what picks the drawings and a fever on the floor
and what the promise holds for other shelters
in a pond. a staple for the marsh that gives
a season in a cloud

its nemesis, like early morning light in the correction
filled with nectar and a blue wheel turning

for the animus the cold makes steady, and a fire
built up in second comings, views—

an opening, round and filled with watchers
in the ocean, in the underside the sand records
beside a snowbound head, on horses and in breathing
still ascensions cycle through the seasons

stops and plays, and magnifies until the cell that empties
gives a visor in a landscape, a blinding hole
lacks answers, in the sparks that settle
fear and burrows in the sand and walks

by planes together with a track and races in a time
unknown, marked by speaking
in a river, in a town, in rain and light that cuts
the hands and far relations float the heart

to a remission, and a war, and hatred making hard
the pools the relatives make red with blood
in summers gone outside the flights, and here
with the allotments a bureaucrat will toggle

in the tension filled with ointments, and a stitch
it hangs the city by the nails, a storm plants fish
for spring in the encroachment floating in a sea of gold
in a dissolving sun, to trade oneself

for solitude and gripping red reminders, in a limb
it feels the need for ghosts, and catches tacks
on hidden photos in the dark, in a relinquishing
inside a fuzzy cloud it loves the noonday sun

and hates the detour that a standing line decides will wait
for gravity and single issue shooters in an arcade
filled with plastic windmills under baskets, and a mute
inside the alien that drops a home into the pools of oil

to grow the blackest door to end the everyday,
arriving with a laughing continental Africa, laments
a toilet stopped with songs, a timely score
messages in each of the arriving temples mark

as holidays and keeping deadly animals, a warning
light pretends, and light discovers, and light
outside the word, inside the hideout
bails of straw keep tongues divided

solved and opened, with rituals and counted fields
beside a head that lost a self, and tunnels in
the story oceans soften, heating the connection
relations view outside volcanic solitude

and the repression that canoes resend in a dissolving rite
makes open each of the Sierras, in a bird
that swims below the light of seeing, a numbness
under vigor in productive calibrations

for a hug. give robotic action for compassion, give the star
an infinite depression that a conversation goes around
in any flower, by the ground that's filled with oil
and seething with good wishes

in a frame it hurts the hand and doesn't know the question,
in alleys for the privacy of functions loose with global

colors in a passing and a bruise, the feelings horses know. a life
is killed to make a shower out of chatter

and carve a predator for absence, in the healing end it settles
captions in a face, and radio announcements
a whale implodes to see. it gives again the picture
filled with static making skin increase the float

and holding out the crowd in its most hated wound that's full
of promises and detours on the way to feel the truth
that never was. graves and candy for the stunted country
gone to fill the sky with perfect poison

here with smiles and number crunching stools. the backdrop
that a crying jag returns for others, for the sea it settles
suns to warm an island, and believes the enemies control
the leisure puddles see in rainbow colors

filling glass. a park, in its sporadic designation, moves with seasons
cities hold for anguish and a vision, making the arrival
of a crowd more like the infant in its helpless curl, a seeing
filled with swollen space

and tender digits, calmly call the others in the ash, the door
that settles visits, openings and dust piles for a love
increasing the amount of volume in a single ring, to hear
a beauty gone to die

arriving, filled with dread and anxious repetition, holding weapons
oiled and loaded, light and strong for killing in the plains
pronounced inside. there is a weaker droning, gone delivery and ice
is stored in empty homes that fade

seen like death it harbors its own limbs and ears
and organs in an echo, in a feeding frenzy
sharks in their exaggerated kindnesses, the slick
regressions tender missiles give

to windows like the light, the pound of meat that stands
to offer gifts in a dismembered warmth, like open secrets
made to power down the boredom, in a woodland
caravan that blackens

shiny ghosts. to be the lesions, all the colors flags undo
and make an integral the power, for announcements
filled with sand and powdered faces in a puppet cell that gives
the meaning of a worm

outside the river city that nostalgia placates and a door
deters to make a welcome of hallucination, salted and undone,
belong in the arrangements younger truth dissolves
and buries in the sky

that harvested the only sentiment, the one intrusion
in the morning nodding out reveals, contusions
filled with earth, inside the web that holds you
to the single stone inside a star

because the story glowing faces roam, settling the wall
in cold at night, the sobbing folded in your skull
and made to last the only call the plastic makes, to settle
for a bus, is here

chancleta

a fear, made of willows, in a gravel park
of punishment and distant voices, plastics do
reveal, in a reception
roads carve into
amplified and brittle
clarity inside the bail of straw
the everyday in its extended segmentation
makes a fall and fills
the lungs with dunes
and luring landscapes
plowed and gone

a certainty alive, a half way house
in its allotment to the bare
makes lamas still and quiet, like a rind
for the alone in snow storms and the true
an anchor for escapes and messengers
hold the hood for night time, like a snake
hidden in a midday sun, targeted
to sell the pockets of a class, a heavy head
writing makes a fool of
tiny sounds of change

an underground resurgence, in the blank
heals highways

and the light, weapons in a glaring
frost the everyday subsumes
for miniscule connected dogs, a walk
increasing in a comet
with a hurt it stays inside
a technical incision, horns of those
i look at
what i see. for each releasing bridge
a flow of iron
into a prison
this, my flower
breaks

for weaker lights and hammocks
for the canine in a visit
for a corn song in the rain
to move a cloud and speak
for empty lots
for numbers

for the frozen body, lost with counseling
the smallest knot
of everyone
in the middle
of the room

for crates and losing pictures
for the worn

for secret meetings, lit inside
for wrongs

for answers in the desert
for relations with a sign
for huts that view the sea
for crying like a deer
for horses in a word
in wooden hearts
and choking necks

for switches in the night
for a rabbit gone to die
for anemones that see
the lost suns
in a river   of microscopic lives
they trill
the whole

for the song in a paper plane
for a tower of shackles
for iraq in its cellular calls
for the hypnotized in a price
the tv bombs
for the pouring rain in a host
for enemies in visions
for the magnet
that you are, outside the light

for the done
in quicksand
for the rattlesnakes
of nature
for those that belong

in a sentence
for the executioners

for the wrongly tied
a number
for the war
in its repose
for the truly light
in the sound
that is wrong
in each of us

for the cactus
and for icicles
for the letter sent
to four corners
the unknown
builds
completions, for the sand
and for camels

for the loud injections
in the mouths
that are inward

for the music
burning carnivals
the heart
for death
for living
in a spiraling error

for the amendment
cut in each accretion
for the pyramid
in a dozen eggs
for the dirt, settled
for answers
and for hay

for the tended clam
and for a twirl

for clinging knots
revealed
in a soapy tongue
for the never ending foam

for a harvest
a criminal
revolves around
for oil
sold for the many
in a *cúmbia*
and each oceanic vomit
in a tropical sweat
the crowd
disperses

for the psychotic flower
a color drowns
and spreads
through light fields

a pair of hands,
the initialized
Runs

i bleed
for the keys
to become, breathless
with a gun
the innocence
condemned to silos
marks

the ocean
does not surround
it does not
extinguish

THE PIER OF SANDY SONGS

chibcha

there is a circle in my name, in the number wheels return
there is a frozen world inside the fear an enemy destroys
its doubt is never gone, except for now. its empty sky is still
along the rivers forests play to catch the darkness

enormous death sleeps still inside the wheel
inside the shoreline people call out to for calmness
in the summer when the houses burn
in the winter blood dissolves

there is a trick to talking to the world, a trick without a mouth
inside abusive absences, the noisy numbers, throbbing
stillness moons refill with oceans
in the deathless light receiving night

there is a language for the count, a wing for blanks
and flights of scrolls in corn fields never ending in the skull
and in the fractured mirror from before that makes me crawl
like snakes with everything

there is a world inside a broken life, like healing with a hanging plant
becoming lost. there is a window to reveal the newness of the sand
and many songs i never sing
eternities of miscommunications

there is a friend for every lover, an enemy for innocence, a condemnation
for the true, a fence for tenderness, a wall

for the unbound and free, a contemplation for the firing squad
and empty poverty for greed

there is a newness to hallucinations in the gravy train embedded in a jaw
a poem for the fossil, nostalgia for the raw in modicums
of celebration, in the gallows fever calls the hole
to liquefy the warmth i never feel, or see, or bought

there is a laughter to the rain, a wound for skies unsettled for a vehicle
in fields of incremental harvesting and pallid growths
and flesh that hides the face for summer to remain
the only exit for a spark

there is a knot for smiles to run the code repeated for a target
in the heyday of a straw man crows believe, for softened
bullets in the handshake filled with springs
together with sincerity, making race belong to rodeos

there is an out of stolen freedom from a word, a copy
memory deceives to be the truth, for bodies in a sea of electricity
diving in a pit of tar to make the world revolve
with endless anonymity, to be

feverish quakes for twins in piles of storage for a word, a queue
remembering a slice of season in the tropics, for plastic in the skin
and balconies above the husk of contact
on the board

there is a knot for every loss of mountains, a landscape filled with future
ruins in the now, a softening regurgitation soaring in a pile
of newer shine and grammar flesh will never fill, a seed
allotments in a room will not make shelter for

there is a flood for the explosions in the horror of a point
in each intention, in the snow it flees direction for the net
and for the ton of weakness tiny knots of goodness
sell for wrong, is still

there is a turning into steel, a resin pulling for the hurt
revolving doors, the glass made into dust believes and heals
a surface done too smooth to walk before
in a derision neuters play for good

there is a stone for quiet rooms in oceans, in the fire
a friendship cuts into for settlements
along the river currents mark for crossing
to the peaks of nothingness

a corpse sings with the holidays and chatters
in the promise presidents revolve around
for deals to sweeten scraps
from all sustaining light in being gone

there is a mark in cures, the bottoms from the tops
in each of the rehearsals for a cell
cut throats to see, in a relinquishing
as tiny towns are floating for the light

there is a slash and burn for necks, petrified in electricity
in halves of swimming toward a birth, in drums
for reasons cut into the garden
growing through the bodies left behind

there is a number in the fields, spanning out the blindness
planting what the ignorance inside me knows

for sitting by the fire for empty promises
turning hemispheres for heat and hurricanes

trembling lovers in the jaws mark up the moon
with trails and beacons in the salt
delivered for a wedding between nuns, the whole
assembled and resembling a war, return the horses

there for stables lit on fire, exceptions
in the body filled with ads and sutures for an age
brings movement to an ash, and hands the foamy eyes
their radios for carving sound and noon eclipses

there for endless distances, a vein, settled down inside a face
of mud filled entryways, the sorry caves for throbbing loss
becomes. live and seed a rattle in the world, a rounded
sea hive pouring through will speak into

and make the shorelines cave to endless rows of thorns
marking repetitions and the wound inside the bleach
deferred for strength in others, drowned for its own self
and cut into the place a home before, another

language in the people that apologies and torture make together
in the pathways on the other side of truth, the side of error
for the way cut through and settled in the snow, a started christ
walks endless surfaces to intersect in time

the reason houses in a prayer, the muffin, wooden
sphere in turns inside a polar bear
with rags dropped into vision
spreading answers to the ground

for seals and weaker drones sand dunes enforce
to make a dozen burials in shells and whitened rooms
they never open, in the heart beat crews
tie down, nine bodies for a door, remain before

for tunnels in the river stalled beside a throat
cut into the tops of heads in ended, in returns
to fill the snow with tracks and mark the insight
in the ground

there is a woven tendril in the arms, they hurry through the distances
marked in undersea ruled souls of facelessness
for coins that shake like visits to a telephone
and not to know the journey into death, with this

there is a beauty smaller stars shine out for moves
and garnish leaderless intentions for the wrong
and places all the horses in a signal in a nighttime
drowsiness feeds into snow

there is a grieving sun extinguished in the middle of the day
a skull leads into forests for the flesh
a reading done with words
rubs out the symbol of a birth in termination

there is a rat for shirting nudes in moss
to cool the burning flesh in winter time
and shiver in the hosts of endless occupations
as a gift of lacking life

there is a promise for the spear arrived inside of those
as any truth is possible where once

the light is made to lie
and twice, the body is not made of blood

there is a service for the long divided in a searing welcome
the placidness a hatred gives to others
for compassion in the never ending war
for the love of balancing the soul in tar

there is a finished sentence for the bullet hearts deny
is there, the ritual in sacrifice of any life
to give the tiny knot its surfacing incorporation
for the infinite in separate losses

then, there is a mound for animals unknown to earth
as they assemble all of us in rockets
for the season of a visitation
in the atmosphere denied, without a cloud

mirror man

the hole
a sign

a time
of broken shells,

here
in rivers

winding
their returns,

assassins
stand with windows
in the profile
of a split reply

on the canopies
of land filled
mines

a hand
an off side
grows
to switch

in the presidential
spillage
viewers in the soil
knot into light

in every tiny
coast
of other ground
velocity, a twin

a line
of greener
tanks
in openings
yesterday
will see,

peeks
into the harvesting
remorse
many were
without themselves
to seem

with rainbows
feeding tables
for a rounder
meeting

like the penetrating
horizontal

moon, begins the end
a fuse
links to
intention—planning
what the people know.

make the host
a water bearer
in the older part
of faces, in the parallel
of singing
burns to shelter
taxis take
for one to be
like waves
with feet
unbound and lost
to people

hosts run down
under a widening
diffusion,
perfect clouds
in airplanes
noon
for sitting
says, a sun

matters like the bread
a picture of deletions
running code

the gutter
in a flash
in mud, denies

for fishing
for the slab
of concrete
that a hearse
makes open
headless—

without rooms
to walk away with

in the intersection
of a town outside
with names
together, like a kite

like the chalk
that scratches
empty cans

into the sea
of never
knowing, in
the promises
a sound

makes ice

the spanish flu

see the palms, the wind denies,
the moon is a just
shelter, for a sinking weight,
pulled to the end
the stars
are borrowed
for carnage, in equations
and promises
the earth moves, a corpse
in its fire
beacons for the sand,
as it starts and belongs
to lost pioneers
and ocean city comas

remind, the ashes are long
and words put inches
on the fields
pocked
with migrations and a tinsel light
in the tar packed up above
the cave in its mines, in its address
will placate and find
in announcements
money makes

for the burn and tear
of planting the end
of houses, as covers
make the engine pilfer it
with trust built to a stop
in buses, for the new
in oxygen
that makes it blue

there never was a reason
for the screen, it marks this page
in squads to fire out arguments,
as the explosion
in a helpless sky, a coast
a plastic vein, its westernmost
activity and light, ready
by the sea, stalled
in turn connected hills
an increase
in the glass filled room
makes cavities
for fingers in the cattle
teeth
return, for courage
and a worm

i walk the field,
a cage is buried in it, the stars
are captured by the sea
a human
makes a canine

will the step
to carve into a number
what the arabic
amends, a pond
burns like the cars
in an arrangement
of a shrine
to light
the crops
with bullets
and a will
to walk along the bridges
that connection
makes a fold
to cold
the handles
of relation
in tropical
departures
for the signs
and words
they make a mouth

there never was
a country
for the house
their particles
in ashes
weave into
as flesh makes
for a wound

emptying
the cities
in a call
in rings
and radios
around the hands
injected
for a season, sills
mark lies
inside the will
of massive
cavities, an entrance
for the seeing
end
for amputation
to begin

even ones
the bleeding
in the snow
cannot remain
or tell
the outer trees
in decimated
hosts, a cousin
filled with lottery
and longing
in the country
one, and four cut through
the flesh
of words

fills in
the corpses
with cold water
and a reason
to remain outside
the food
revealed
to be a light

i imagine
lines
a chest
will break
refusals
for a civil war
on wooden
rafts, containers
of the object
in a binding
coast,
a rack, the egg
makes horses
this returns, gives in
the poles
and older songs
receive alarms
the children
see

the frost
in lonely handshakes

in a city full of bells
is never finished
in the polar wind
and digs within
a wilderness
for more than many
know to end
the cold

first languish

the signal came for walking, in remembering, the parched and never
done, a landscape healed with multiple revulsions, a service
to the ice instead of worms, the green becomes the hole the others see
outside the machinations viewers call for, in a vacuum

it is here, the trail from dot to dot, the grasslands tickle
storms. turn around the deathless, a new root in a lion's
cold resurgence, in its misery, when hard as steel and on the line
workers in the rain record, is

a magnifying icicle moves timeless doors to passages, quick
inside illuminated insects, divisors peel a natural skin
from roads in bushes, a doctor cuts through clouds
to shine and bear the inside of a plan to see the sun again

lacerated bodies piled into a course, a serial connection winter beds
fleeting in the increase by a window, for the tropics and a numinous intention
a snake man in the snow makes yellow colors for, and marks a red interior
for patterns smearing in the rain

the husk of segmentation land, a newborn dread of microscopic dreams
searches pioneers, the last land cities maul, arrivals words call out for
growing light, to make the end of toggling, lonely for the small,
yeses plant for welcome, for the tarot

under sand—where children play. a freezing in a frame, the one
a trade all languages can come before, a sharpened sight made into space

a city in its calls to the encroaching cockroach, makes to shed
the tears, to quench the thirst of others

this landscape is the prison dreams equate with sadness, that the sadness
never knows, in its replies to services unanswered, in the offal
thick trees sink their deepest roots into, to serve the air and be the home
to birds that know the songs to move the wind to clear the sky

for rivers bridges cave into, for fish to swim to mark the ground
below the water with the answers for necessity
making poems for machines to make the same as tenderness and vile attention
filled with trouble for the road

in harvesting equations of the moon, a brittle sky made black
for pock marks in the empty stare filled night with hills
blocking stars and shining with the dew, for fish of never knowing
burying the bulges in the ad bombed out for mercy

in the need it swells the energy in sick days in the fire marking a room
to shoot inside with seals and suns and boats, in silent aviaries
throbbing with the deadly plans and circles in the words put twice together
in the cavities i fill with tar

a tiny laugh marks flesh with cold responses, in the mountains
herons in their deathless white will shadow first of all, with feathers
guiding each of every end for a reception
in the last days of your song

and then a pond breaks shadows in the summer
and increases mountains on the ice cut into endless
travels in the earth, inside an alien contusion light begins
with moles delivered like a time warp for the mob

in blackness days belong to, in blinding reddened hugs
the sun delivers for a people lost in their most hardened stances,
like a mushroom, like the welcome oceans make for bodies lost at sea
like fire for stars they make a memory of leaves

i remain a Host, a pregnant password marking posses
in endless endings searching out the lost in each of us, like lies
it marks my nails with tiny clouds, and like an apple
dropping hard down from the sky

this impregnates the horizons with another sun, the sun of empty circles
filled with enemies and emptiness, filled with hurt and blossoming
incisions in alarms and in the plains they settle
borders for a line of grace

except the bison in connection, in the fever toggles make for light
outside the round and open door it makes me breathe,
which time i'll never know, a miracle makes circles round machetes
for the slash and burn inside the necks they promise this

a desiccated hand filled mouth, the breath is harvested alone
without a promise to reveal what integrated circuits know the patterns
conversations hold, the ointment settled in the noise, that swells with fire
a state bleeds holes to see

weaker for the motion gates in their two sided plant, a strategy
builds snow to house the weak, a separate self in the attachment
floods a sense of answers in the trouble mountains hold
in the allotment for the isthmus in a warmth

for the releases in the warning tunnels in a seeing eye can feel
and stomach the approach to meteors for hands upheld

to carve the wood into a nest, the shadow in a corn filled frenzy
murders fill with fantasy, and newness, and intend

to open for the grains of sight, the window cracks in the ascension
strings amended for the wavy lines marking relational
appearances, a sewer digitized and ready for the clean
heightened numbers in the crowded stadiums

for registers they claim the first of these ignited hands
and seal a density unsolved and sold or served
to the release of scarred retention, like the lake
it cradles death

and like the momentary place in tune with what's forgetful,
in the mountains ringing guides into the snow
for quiet in climbing days revisited, to find the stone
that sinks another heart

with each of the atonements, in the side a two equates
with feathers, in the easter bonnet cities mark
to fill the breath with an arrival to the rodeo
and sing the ropes injecting light into the night

for sending and receiving in the meat the others hold
forgiven for the spider's web it marks a dying flight
of enemy remorse, the wound breathes synchronized
with all the ants that run

and in the fight of targets fur resends
in circles in the blinded good, a rounded
road brings violence in to others
in the weeping light turns on

a horse will never know the saddle, the snow
believes the day is started for the steel and cold
beside the bed it startles dolls to sleep, a doll
it never knows the life of its own self

for groups of heads and legs selling the street, for moss
the lakes in the attention of a shade remember
under ancient villages, the soaring staff heals up
a self-dismembered man

there is a newness to the noise inside, a whistling bird of white
it never dies, the laughter in a mammal parks
equate with sadness, a cutting steel knows onions
in the city of a scab

when automatic sessions, in the pose of selling computation
a smile the information harvests for the bitter root of light
in a reasoning of plastic and a noose making itself
the end of plans

then, the seasons die, the sun equates the moon
with faces, the light inside becomes a field of burning
letters to the ground. give the end another welcome
as a place where sadness becomes space

and all the feelings are like fingers, gone to while the time
to make the loops in all the pallid plastic, in the sun
and make a reason fold into the end
and come to wake the morning full of mud and steel

cage fight

you thought that necks
were virgin, like the sea
that once divided
stars

you thought she was alone and still
after the knife across
the river, in the mountains
under streams of soil

they grow the seeds. the quick
in burning coats, and dances
snakes wrap in the dark,
will capture

frozen eyes
the sprays of reddened
words and pasts along
the canyon, still and carved.

she makes the rain pour down
the bloody limbs on apple trees
sands move over
in the hospitality of enemies

within a war the numbers count
in buses riding on eclipses
sliding rocks into the bell
it fears the insects in the season

of an underground return. the pace
in shells of planting pinkish flesh,
mornings call to start a rose
beside the error, fear

inside the window of a plane
instead of bombs, is what the other
neck collects to end the slashes
by the love of her last sound.

the first of all the dying birds
along the trails in visions of a host
tear down its own four sided room
inside the rabbit hole it makes

a reason end with slaughter. what
the honest and the vile and stitched
up road, in hollowed bodies
like the squirt inside savannas

in a house it halves its memories
to wear the promise of the flesh. a deer
makes warmth of tiny bodies stop
within each family

dissolves beside machine guns, in the grocery
within the first days of a show. speak
without an understanding of the word
that ends, the word the nets cut into

hatching blossoms on the battlefields
beside the flowers birthday boys
will execute with smiles. passing on
a white cell in a poem full of sparkles

with a love of petals rearranged to sell
the color of a storm, and the number
of compassionate electrocutions, by the last words
of a letter making homes

of healing pucker in a catastrophic
case of easy starts. what can bear the little
words, parades of revolution
in the air filled up with clouds

in touch with rainy days they make a nail
for thirst and water. in the air
it does not picture its intent
outside the promising correction

of a view, of ice inside the fraction of the cost
of seeing red as written. each and every mouth
makes the best of its relation, in the money
of a cart it pleads with shopping

in tornados, the west of her intention
in the tunnel in her throat, can make to others
what a death inside a word by day will know. when
the ball of light speaks out to twins, when music

in the evening of the exit of the time
neighbors make a word sit still, inside
the dirt filled mouth lips move together
with the town the people in their boxes, on

the screen it peels itself from lightning
to the cloudy mark it makes invisible
what ants come home to do. they can hurt
the little people in the little trains

and make the little papers that will make
you miserable, in each of my dead faces
full of mouths they stab into the lungs
of nothing but the breath. split the message

in a rainy day it tears the tears in two.
when the man inside a bathroom stall
with two feet on the ground, can place
the lines drawn out, a rope from eye to eye

to walk the circus from the room
of stale revolvers, and, of resignation
from the shriveled pulsing raisin
people know, the dots across

the river getting started with the first disease
and ended with two eyes removed. to walk
among the cut–outs in the woodland
state they never knew the light of bodies

the smaller countries in the field
of time machines were meant to be.
the shape of endless trials, forgiven,
for the end of tyrants in a bud they never

knew the sun, its gradual unfolding
in a point in space is breathed upon
from far away, will make again
each shape it moves itself through series

from a sphere to anything and back again.
as a murder can be wired,
to push an end through broken screens,
a cactus growing from a pool of doubt.

•

the sevens are the morning
a service in the daisy chain
of hanging fruit, discarded lives
will blame you for. directions

to the northern fate of termination
and the centered dip into the oil
it stops the wheels and makes the toneless cry
for terror, for the sidewalk still

to carry on the flesh the food equates to weapons
digging the interrogation
for relaxed and targeted
eruptions of a breath. what can it remember

storming through the circles
in the forest fauna
a plastic face can move into the light?
this leak for hate that bleeds

revolving door

the mailman never came without a warning
i look into the freezer full of lost survivors

nutrients angle up the days into a parking lot
they run outside my crowded hands with trails

the winter comes inside a daisy chain of greetings
for rocks to build a waterfall

each number clouds forget to wet
remains beside the grasses in the colors of a kite

a window pools of blood intend
is fishing out the everyday with calibrations

a tree that stretches into space
is rooted for a fever twins cut into clay

an animal that does not hear a word
is grounded like migrations in the wind

a head falls down without a family
and now it calls the love of life a telephone

inside the paper cup the towns desert
begins a spring for bottled breath

without a driveway for deliveries to enter into homes
a square is split with circles

outside the network that a child believes is god
return the ranches that a saddle rakes into the ground

the city never writes inside for less than services and wood
and now the coasts equate the links between the roads

their towns carve trains without a sound
dissolve, and make a fleet of robots fall

as keyholes do what nights reflect
and start the hands in digital and calm dissent

and when the speed of eyesight in the endless stacks moves to the top
the bodies armies hide are pushed into a blush

however empty the attentions of a crime
a laser spiral plows a piece of land and eats the eye

inside the minerals, piling up a dog
grow tiny gifts the lonely singers throw into the dust

inside the endings fronds make tropical
warms a shelter wicker baskets hold iguanas in

beside a prison that the other side of silence burns
sit rows of costumed guards that sway with never ending calls

along the frozen welcomes families of bureaucrats receive
runs a hand that stitches its intention for a fall

around the age old suicides forgotten for the ride inside a bomb
turn solid tokens for the hammer thrown into a park

within the starlight that the power of an absence pushes into yesterday
anonymous and grinning fathers turn the square of faces into light

the calculation carnivals rely upon is reached
as joyous births kick carcasses into the muddy trials, a three

water goes with fours and shoots the morning full of night
in daylight passing for the wrong

as a network is heated up, my line of urine hooks up to the sea
a charge goes through me

as the world is read
as it might be done

as the lines are lost
as it was said in two for light

as a one remembers digits, a face a gate
as a pier remains

as the antelope
as the crossing through the wall

as a river of a heart becomes
as a hub for lightning bolts

as the ground
as signs are left

as the sticks make dragon flies
as a bundle

of sticks
as it is again

as the arrival of a body
for a sun to open

as the repair the others make
with flying

as the reminder
as a wing

as it is gone
as it is here

as the breath
as a word sits through it all

as the fear of skin
as it is written on a door

as the morning
will not be wrong, together

as the 12
stars
of the world

as the 3
elements
of a new place, the crisp
night a gaze
makes into light

the wind
of a color
like a clear
day—is
not red, the most
skies were
to see
a breath, the thrown
together place
an entrance, a doll
eats shit
to clear and see
the two moons, the ride
a key, for silence
is open

a path
she knows

the double
is moving

to converge
the two

elemental song

a shadow scraped, the negative
is answers, seeking solace
in the long ways of a shiny bridge

a fur sparks into graves
the outside visitations
around driving

a cycle starts delivery
of braided water, each seat
stays still for the disaster tree

a thorn pricks parching gardens
famished and worn
a moon arrives in a soft absorption

a knot erases what preceded it
the pier is closed
and each hill is pulverized

for the reflection that a face
is indivisible
with grammar and a husk

the number on a tag
the marsh that fades
each ghost that the mark

equates with eggs, given what
the machine makes
for another, a green field

is not what a question is, the reply has
what a placid
street that a girl gives, to the forgiven

with it saddled, in the city that is down
to heal a body's cage
its disease is to rest

incrementally, night is cold and the tapes
in each crowd that the shells are
to sea

grown, not a hollow for each
that stands and minimizes
a father, each one that a table

has delivery for, steps, the rule
that has the extra flesh
for its widest engine, the halt

forward, lengthening each road
inside, inside the tree nest
gone to it, as time's single eye

to the person, the line out that a grieving
less a suddenness, a rain that has
a first day gone, for lights out

that peels each hand, a finger for
10 times a trial, the field that has
no palm to make a plug, a surge

for the superimposed, the arrogant
widened body of law
that a hand makes for each that is assured

that the day begins, that the season
plants with its own corruption
to make signals and return

a hole that the hill is dense with, each lock
undone to the wire
to the floating force that tribal gates make

for nothing. what shines, the one
called less in groups
in the seasonal crying that blue gives

to the inside dust, in the corn
that beads out with horses
to coins

for rain, for a marriage
in the rising flood, for night
to pulse the headlines

that a rate, a forest, each miniscule
ash, that a hand
in easter, for the rain can give

to each end of its own, of the song twin
that a maker is to move to, for the aisle
in bridges that a soap can make in this

in this that a wearing is to light
and to the radio that is not
when this is to give

and the given to the other, the field
that green is to its killing
in the season that a peaceful place

snow has to its length added, its room
filled for operations
to its floor that a sail is

gone to one another, another telephone
for these, for the soon
that has no place, no hands

in a room that is packaged, to its hue
to the place that has
a rotted skin spread out

a number cut into an open hand
its magnet to its one, to call
as the human gone

to zero, to remember clouds
that seem stalled at the tolls
given the mother of

connection. a corn field right for now has
in the tulip twice to the morning
for the road in its purchase

that has to a real engine that is
gone to a host, the web is
the settled that no one makes

in each that a moon increases to it
to the mile high sign
that a spoon that makes time in a picture

and to the radial that has its own in the ice
gone to it, to the seeping that has
in the gone that a super has to know

in the door, in the increasing cloud that points
in the gone together
to the wrong in the wrong in the right

to each that has its own, in the face
of the each that has as its own
to a given in hands and the own

and the own given that each has
in the sold, in the given twice
that has the tone that has its one

in the given each to each in the face
that has tones, in the light of its
to go the light of its, in the one

and the one that has its time in the only
in the place together with it in its
when there is to one a second time

and the place has the door that belongs
to it that is in the place over in its light
time to the arrival of one place to its one

and the line that has its one to give
in the arrival to it is one to the only place
that has as its one is the only place together

and the one has to give it as the one to give
and given to each hand and the place
to the only time that has one to give

in the one place that has one to the others
and the one that has its place gone
and given

ATLANTIS AND THE OCEAN OF BLOOD

the price of pain

when a salamander
turns a palm
in hands
of wood, instead
of breathing
visits
on a plane
its steps
will leave,
around the planetary pools
one like one decides
to give, a root
a fallen part
of you

the water
green and lost
around an excremental
star—sheets of ice
put points to follow
each volcano
lines horizons
for a tuft
of lightning flashes
by the cursive

on the egg
that starts
to sweat

the many, in relational
a row of tags
for buttons
push, the trunk
for flashes
for a limit
branches
for a shore. claws
remain outside
the street
in entrances and fall
into the palms
of cupping sounds
for spines
to grow
to light
the leaves

servicing the night
a count
for holes, a hole
makes life-lines
by a spring, a bathing
goat—to move
the castle covered
by the wind
is blossoming

in devils
sleep intends
to put together
with a people
and a negative
inside

doors
are driven
for extensions
in a fire,
a cage
stretches out
in each revision
to a limb
shriveling
with noonday
suns, a face
to ward off
nighttime
walls and balances
the wings
of deathless blanks
Return

an etched out
grave, a wood
that severs
each rejoining
each ascent
to place the cave

inside arrested
currents
by the window
for reflections
crack
the price
prosthetics give
to amplify
a hardened
bead of rain

the surplus
of an anchor
on the shore
is raw
and makes the palms
run off
in graceful fences,
bitten down
like patterns,
like a road
inside the lit up
dirt
to give the light
a pulse
around the question
fruits
will leave

when aviation
sings to other

lines
a cross
of dust, switches
terminals
to enervate
a body count
to make the fastest
of a fisherman's relays,
a flood
it promises
a pier

ceremonial regressions
put along the skins
what one decides
to make a digit
in a life
give out
in fields
in llama caravans,
to help the static
make a tendril
for a splattered
decimal
a one
can give
to each
release and feed
a palm
in separate bits
together
for a limb

el moro

they were out beyond
the eggshell, of the road

the whitened foam
the bars
in keys
measure out
a hollowed earth
and translate
into silence

as it pours
outside the trace
and carries out
contractions
to the westernmost
infinity
that fuels the end
10,000 years before.

it breathes again
to see a self
swallowed up
built up in skies
collapsed upon

a beacon
terminated night.

a skull inside
is written on
and full of cuts

a hunt dissolves
to ruin
random visits
in the country
of a flattened out
reclusion
in the dust

the summer
in the winter
of the carrion
is once, and once
moved in
to sleep
inside the body
of a double
mute
within a house
that's crumbled down
in water
others mark
for death,

here to trade

the state of opening—
a candle
for the air
as steel removes
to climb the walls
cobblestones
increase, a coldness
for erasure
and a wreck inside
the bones
the streets endure
for feet

anonymous
attached
fatalities
in loops
they iterate
for land

                fear puts down a stalk
                    a spherical arrest
           for wings, an outage
            of disintegration
                 for a word
                      it travels
                  from equators
                        to the hands
                            and lines the bottoms
                  of the oceans

                        a desperate
                  renaming
                        of a guest. deliveries
                        make promises
                              a hardened
                              glacier
                              in the entrance
                              for a piece full out
                              of pointers, in the season
                              where the breath
                              is held to herds, and even
                              in the pocket

of a cloud
the radiation
climbs into for nothing
in a husk
wrapped up
in ancient words, not gone
connected
to a ring, in separation
rites along the eye
if meaning comes
to warn
the rain, the ruined
crowd. a table

by the mailbox
fields give lines
to horses, in a grid
it places markers

for a sentence
for a hill, a row
for making services
a drum, not ever
for the fleece. shelters
in a port,
the protocols
an enemy
will act upon, on days
a silent flight
makes talons
for a stop
to mean a will
will never
end a pattern
– town, a slope
dissolves in two
horizons.

a flood
the empty caravan
remains.
the fields
of skeletal replacements
sorry crisis
tiny waves of shame

and intimate
in signs, a softened
batch of handicaps
regards within

a space
exploded
through the night

cockroach

make a letter line a cloud, and sleep, and make a wound
another planet stretched with skin, the news plants beads and pierces
fields, another suture in the air between us, glowing words
they pull a bag over the head and guide the sparkling snow,
dogs under the oceans pulling chains to drag a whiteness
to the one, a hearse rides out for strings in automatic
recognition of the armies stiff with cartoon beggars, the healed hang down
inside the trailer light reveals for checks. there is no passive door
to seal the halo, exploding in a warmth on fire for creases in executive
balloons, corrugated roofs throw shines to know the sounds of words,
bodies in the picture of the rest, no one breathes in but to survive
a network in the shattered cross in circles with a meaning for a mouth
settling the desert, filled with selves they draw four separate maps
and move without a forward step, soaking up the water in a comfort cell

there is no window for the force of errors, any air goes out the tracks
and makes its newborn vinyl like a broken moon, a saddle for the one to one
recursive eyes that flower out eruptions in return, with politics
they skin the smallest animals for night time vision, *apagado*, filled with numbers
in the snow it runs into the trees, to cross the ice all flattened out
and wiring, this, the memorized in mountains, in the earthquake
greetings slice into the buses for a morning in a palm. a leg
refills the cabin in a function sewers hold outside the light, with travel, built
to hub the sun and stare at storms inside the cloth the cotton once lit up
for walks throughout the sounds of execution, clicks instead of ends
along with oceans of a chance through doors they cradle up the egg of witness
in the cloud it crashes for a newer time. there could never be another

gate to ping itself inside a meditation fire, its country settled for okays
and for surveillance, each of the intentions of a worker for the warmth

around the target coming down. a hike into elastic vistas, like horizons
in the rubbermaid attire, horns point to the only path
with ancient rubble in a flea torn shore at night. west of the revised
attachment, in a hand it flattens out the dust in trembling
for a house under the heat, in drops of drying blood
and makes a roof for fingerprints, the faces in an ashen chest torn open
mute for counting tables borrowed in the northern sight
of matrimony, selves together for a solitude that swells a sponge
in sounds ignited by a sharpened stick, the forest makes a hole
inside the cash negated for a ring. deadened time in the allotment stolen
for a burn, the star undone for others
as a sacrifice, the death of cheap replacements
on the people trade that one of these is meant to keep, the blind
in recognition, darkened knots keep names together

for a run. the plane of questions in a vacuum empty of its word
relays in a projected kind of country, in the Spanish
cave it knows the name of others for a hive, the dogs
returned to the iguanas in a clearing, in a crack filled noontime
seasons mark inside a breath, ascents
recorded in a blank, a flood
heats numbered wind and carries life
along the travel nakedness will iron out in a fire—
no warrant, not a rising elevator for the voice
it carries. bleeding, the rejected and the crispiness of night
outside a prison in a smile, a hill
of throbbing coals they never warm the sleep of fear
in each of the adornments for a rite
or standing tall outside

the sewer
of a lesser hand, a bit
that settles in
a rose, beside the ashes
mouths move out, following
the rivers on
the head of any
lake filled for a cloud with foam
in each loop of a song.
it falls and rests
to one the eyes have
in a washing
pier, certified, like hatred

under it, the segmentation
rivers in a knot
a horn the social aches
revisit, in the boiling
waver frozen faces
eastern rattles, threats
that never end, beside
the husk i make into
a living, a time erased
like heartbeats
that battalions, in their breathing
what the bitter stone
a forest in the ad
on fire, for killing you. be

the freedom opening
a torture garden
in your valentine. because

a hangman stops
to visit the forlorn
in their equations
testing code, the passionate
in manikins, the crying jag
a screen erupts in
being blue. it never knew
the ruling of a court
in scars
its weaving through the fear
it makes a home

be still, like leaden weights
in the atonement
of a dying fish, the loaves
make cactus flood
the deserts full of friendly
cloth and covers
what the horses
in their dying, for the snow
remove to make a shield
another head
that carries soft deliveries
abandoned, in a heartache
not a country
or a road, a synchronized

retirement from the grave.
each double, in the loam
drowns silos
full of fingers,
ghosts collecting what was thin

in slashes, like the harm
that settles in the day
for pockets full of headless
force betrayed for eyes,
see knives
my circulation makes
to breathe again, and cut
the softened head
from each of the resurgences—

to own a zero, and have light
together, with a plane
in endless hallways, in a city
blights within
a shirt, in rounded gifts
that people plant
to grow outside the winds
to make a space, a neutral
heat of put together farms
for networks to remove
the information in a bloodless
life, without a body
in the endless war
of filling faces
with the time
of done
with nothing
in this ever
gone to end, the water
wheels
to see

black horse in the snow

a never ending day
has stitched the light
with paths, in a return
of anthills building up
the sky in fast robotic
sentences that plant the many ends
of firing squads, a heat wave
windows hold to ease
the massacres
and stones belonging
to the names of dust.
an empty skull is the attention
a hurricane will toll
the ashes for escape

to move the sleep from weapons
and bury what will throb
with language lost
together with the knotted hands
that carve my name into the ground.
a door hides what will make an empty sun
another opening
for leaving in a frenzy
what relations end with numbers
thawing out the ice, it stops a vision

pushing endless planets
in the moonlight that the porous
wills to an incision
filled with zeros and a one.

i look at beauty, and it dies
synchronized with love
is the periphery,
poking out with guns.
a murmur in the heart comes up
with flapping flesh
and slashing she
who makes a home
for us, with what ive managed to become
with breathing, in the hollow head
that ends with exhalations
putting knives to naked skin. what
have i survived to be, if with a word
i think the wrong i always fight
is right for me. i bring it out into the world
and go, to make
and not to see—

to move the moon inside the sun. a black horse
in the snow
was there in front of me
and then was gone, it remained
in front of me
and then was gone. i walk
and put together snow and branches
feasts of broken flesh

sit there and announce
the flight of others, in the innocence
of animals that seek
an end to this
that i am human now
eruptions on horizons
severed fingers cannot touch

the radio encircled songs
build a bridge between the scabs
to reach out for the rope
that hung me as a youth, and burn
the night time fire
apologies for everything
a shell marked up with muted words
outside the only face
a half way house is warm enough
to shadow in the calling
that the other heart
the one of making
with a word, a saddle in the rain
cuts through the mountains
for a season that is dead
inside will see

the multitudes that see
that we are one
in light, a spring that kills the air
for missiles redirected by a ball
to run the holograms in seeds
in hosts that start

from coasts and spaces
once, like stars that navigate
to split, remembering the sun
itself the end for what breathes in
the oceans and the time
knotted up and thrown from speeding cars
and run for speaking
without wait, the nuisance
of a soul the power knows is blanking out

it blanks with pools
of moonless palms, the scorpion
injects the desert into open eyes
from other galaxies, the ones
that parch the soil
to make an ocean flood through rivers
in a mushroom that the sky devours
with a body that communicates
the muted sky at night
for thunder that will reach
your heart, and cut it
with a bolt of light, and make you twice
the one that starts
the planes

the ended life that settles
in a weekend for alarms
each of the attritions
in the skeletal remains
of life, blanks out itself
to wear the ghost

that never spoke, the friend
in silence that is sliced
remains, to hear explosions
under masks, with dogs
that leash humiliations
for the crawl i am to be
again, erasing what the light
has burned

there is no repetition
in the explorations
two to make a wrong
the jungle given for the bread
in these aquatic scales, the slithering
for slowing down in winter cold
returns to glimpses in the darkness
under ground, the flash
that suicide rejects
for fleeces that the ancient
wars push out
into the sun, to wear the promise
that a heat connects
and *guayaberas*, in their fruit
become to warm the spider hole

a shelter
in the earth, a bomb
that fills the day with light
like hands pulled out of gloves
the blood that sticks
the camps together

for the vine that breaks a wall
and brings the air
into the egg
that's ready, for a trip
of ending trailers
in the crowded
snakes that fill the sky
with eyes

recursions

shell, maker of your days and nights
alarms are the arrangements of an ocean
troubled by the light, the salt
peels your face into the sky

what carcass does the road display today
to be the life
like snow, in drifts attacking
choices in a dot, a telepathic hunt—

the ripple of a bit floats up in stereo
a hurt the white cells can combine
to make an airy refuge
for explosions in a silent, grazing fawn

newer than the tar it heats the middle
of a cracking sag, the robes
grow centers for the cactus
in the dirt it clouds the eyes of infants in the sun

for dolls to make their way into the room
el cuarto lleno de piel
el cuarto sín ruidos
una vida de teléfonos colgados

dime la palabra que nunca se llena de polvo
conejo
emplumado
conejito

i arrive to the snow on a plane
a bridge a not in the night
a vacuum
in a throb of flowers

this together on a slip
holds a truer visit, by the rain
along the rivers sprawling out the homeless
in a rhythm flood is made together by

systems glow a lack of one, a map
of outside doors, checked off and ready
for the razor and the knife belonging to the sight
of lesser nights together with a byte

to make a way of separating number from a mouth
to sleep with counts and avenues
on springs in ruins
of a metal face carved up with paths

and splitting wood, the sounds of northern, cut
a management of bread
the slow disaster in a dawn of isolations
heals the only heart and sells the zeros out

the blood of seeing. nothing walks for enemies
the aim of missiles and a marshmallow

for countries small with venom and a bridge
to mark the ending of an ant

walk the isthmus and you see

walk an isthmus in the trouble that is gone

erasing the before the others were

on the asphalt up again, the thorns

are clutched for palms

rested up, and feed the openings

to quake, the shame the colors

field with illnesses, in rosy coffins

resurrections in a target

at a mile marked up in air for momentary

Help, a growing husk for each of the alignments

in a softened block of lead

makes a welcome passage for the light in tiny suns

a possible reception, cheery adolescents

in her visitation to the true, the giant, and the angle

in a daylight compromise, together

with your sense of apparition, in a home

the rest of nectar follows

and flows to be in leaves that touch

the rays in your remembrances. i capture all the views

settled on the way to wind

and mean a tremble in the combine of the faces

fallen for a hut

in water, in the circuits, for the ease

of targeting a star,

extinguishing the flesh it makes a landscape

for the central interventions

in the ice and numbs the free. what free, to you

means in slithering delivery

ascension to the arc of anchors thrown to sea

reversed for an anatomy in motherboards

a pull the undertow designs for couples in a blank

between us, for the circle in a lost horizon

like a temple newer mutilations

in a service for the enemies and Hosts

of networks seeking an identity

a current in the light years of a visitation

a face in its rehearsal for a smile,

a valuable response to microscopic platitudes

inside the wind it settles on your voice, the voice

of tender care and battle guns

forgiven by a force of happiness

a house tied up with hangmen

for the promise in a shiny world, a flash

that i belong to, in a super calibrated

greeting for the softness, touch

your hand as axes fall

to end your parasite of goodness, in the weekend

full of flattened out returns

of piling in the leaves to count obsessions

like the trees, and grow for daylight

for the night it makes a nest

inside the offal and the down

of each atonement, in a promise

a body cut in many pieces

like the pixelated, for getting on with credit

in the service life reveals

for death in two

tleta ketama

there is no mud place, any more
melilla is there by the side
of the mountains
stretching two nights
to arrive with an african goat
in a chase of moroccan descent
to deliver a packet of light

overseas, in the poison
let go in the urine
to move to the station
before the thick walls
and the steel
grow
with a hole in the mouth
of a worm, in the shower
foreseen by a blizzard

for the husk
in a country that's selling
a grateful return to the atlas
pulling out fish
in a fever that's marking
these planets inside

for a cell
and a window
erased in a desert
becoming mirages
and hurt by the sound
in an earthquake of seals
in a series of blanks

for the scent
of anything wet
to fill in a shell
in a morning that's bulging
with straw
in a heat making sand

for a season of pleasure
in thorns
marked by pennies

for a voyage that turns
to a heart as a server
with violence in switches
inside in a clearing
deserted by humans

in a skull making rain
in an orbit
surrounding cicadas
and weeping
with silent erasers
a forest unknown
to the light

driving in networks
settling roads

for alarms
in a signal, buried

a host of a wound
in the ocean
disgusted with salt
on a seahorse
riding for flowers

cut into the arm
of a cross in a circle
collapsed
like a bug

receiving reception
a social
in isolate eyes
the war in a face
on a tongue in the cold
in relation to buttons
like hair
on a model, frozen

for money
and vision
in counts
for a zero

and turns with a one
near easter

and rain for the worst
a wheel turns to see
become ready

a crack
in the ground, for the hand

repairing arrivals
in recursive
intents, by a voice
in the rapid
exchange of a bit, a cold
the summer tornado inhabits
balloons with a void
in the palms—

even the trail
where the bones of a bird
in the quickness
that crosses a field, the moon
in a snake in the spring
in a horse moving blackness
in snow on the wood
for a century gone
to discover the faces, the hair
in a knot holding couples

for service
for networks made open
the water in towns in decline
in a sky
where a crane and a magnet
filled with the rain
again in the shadows
with knives pushing out
the turn of the sun
with a face
underground, with a winter

unknown to the native
restored with the light
with a thorn making water
through windows
betrayed by the speed
breaking shells,
for recursive
two twins
with a digit
in each of the planets
in orbits

making a word
and for being
two wheels
on a bridge that is one

ashen earth

there never was a day
that the head of a rosy
remote, under lamps
so sickness was rooted
is still
in a silence and sewing
two tips and two countries
a cut and a plane
in a reason bloomed out
like a cannon
that humans receive

a day made to settle

destroyed by a word
in a knot
like a choice
that is frozen, for nature

revealed like a death
with a music
like birds
falling and landing at night
where darkness is solid
and flesh, like a host

continues the sentence
for hatred and ends

it is there.

less for the sunlight, eclipses
reset for a morning
the contrast
a self made for answers
two worlds that are born
from afar.

from the nearness
that points
to the sun.

from the heart
of a stone
in the mouth

of a manatee
speaking

for oceans
inside the arrival
of islands

marking horizons
undone by the fear
of explorers

ending the weather
peeling off skin
of a body that's quaking
with mental incisions

a mountain
sheltering moons

in the kiss
that is always an isthmus
and planted
in season with pictures

to play in the daydreams
burning up storms
of a door

in a face
that is mine
for another

in an arm
arising
for measure

in a leg
that is still
for the worms
in the earth

in a heart
that is black
with arrival

and alight
with the morning

in a sex
like a kettle,
like thorns

in each
of the animals

crossing
electric
horizons

in islands
on top
of volcanoes

filling each breath
with the sand

of the water
clearing the eyes

of two oceans
two countries
two skies

embracing
the long
made of two
in the loneliest

length of an arc
of the star
that is settled

for light
in the space
that is love

acknowledgments

Some of these poems first appeared in *antennae, Brooklyn Rail, Crayon, Chicago Review, Court Green,* and *Fascicle.* "elemental song" appeared as a chapbook by Answer Tag Home Press, in 2006. Many thanks to the editors. And thanks especially to Jesse Seldess, who was a major force in my life during the time these poems were written.

bicycle was written in two years of a four-year period in which I rode my bicycle 20 miles, meditated an hour, and wrote an hour each day six days per week while also working full-time. I missed, perhaps, three days per year of this routine. And so I rode through thunderstorms, snowstorms, 20-degree-below-zero weather, all kinds of extremes, and one thing I learned was that there is always someone else out there. Through this practice I also learned to relate to the landscape, the sky, the pier, and the lake in a nameless and ancient way. This book was complete in 2006.